TRIUMPH

PICTORIAL HISTORY OF THE GREAT BRITISH MARQUE

Running in water, 20 minutes without a stop.

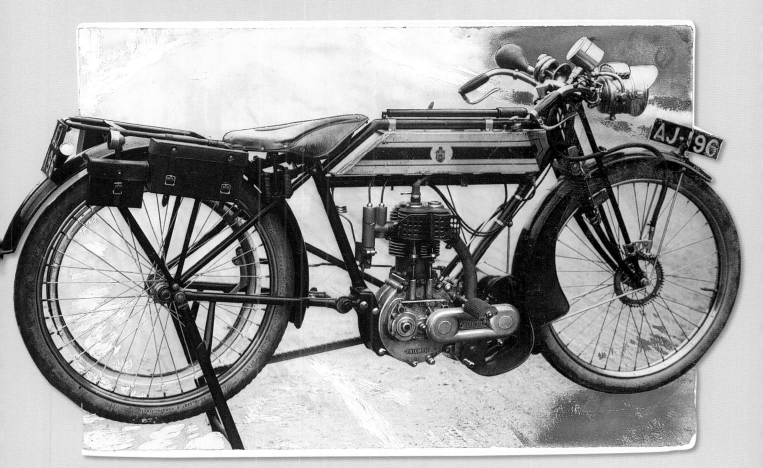

Single speed with acetylene lights, 1910.

JH Watson, November 1910.

advantage over Schulte. The Coventry-based firm now, rapidly, went from strength to strength. Schulte, particularly, had an interest in motorcycles and was keen to branch out into powered two-wheeled manufacture. Meanwhile, Dunlop had been impressed by the company and persuaded Harvey du Cros to invest a whopping £45,000 in the Triumph concern. No longer was Triumph a struggling minnow – the company was becoming a big player in the two-wheeled world and the natural progression was into motorcycles. In 1902, Schulte fitted a Belgian-built Minerva engine into a Triumph cycle and the first Triumph motorcycle was created. Belgian company Minerva was at the time regarded as among the best units available and though JA Prestwich (JAP) and Fafnir proprietary engines were used, by 1905 Triumph was making its own engine in-house. It was a remarkable progression – in just three years Triumph had progressed from bolting an engine to a cycle frame, to a producer of complete motorcycles.

The key thing was that as well as becoming established quickly, Triumph built a good product. The first Triumph engine was a 363cc side-valve, for which 3hp was claimed. There was nothing flash or complicated about the engine – it was just well engineered and carefully put together and soon the

1906 3hp.

Triumph reputation was growing. By 1907, a 453cc engine was being made – that was upped to 476cc in 1908, then 499cc in 1910. Meanwhile, though, a second design of engine was also introduced to run alongside the initial motor. At the first Isle of Man TT in 1907, Triumph's Jack Marshall and Frank Hulbert finished second and third in the single cylinder class – a result that Marshall improved the next year, winning the class on what was possibly the world's first purpose-built racer. Other endurance runs, including the Reverend Basil H Davies' (aka Ixion) 200 mile epic in 1906 and then the efforts of Ivan Hart-Davies and Albert Catt, all helped to ensure Triumph was well and truly on the map.

JR Haswell, TT practice, June 1912.

Aircraft flypast, 1914.

Baby Triumph, 1914.

Mr and Mrs CC Cooke of North Mimms, Hatfield – 3hp models.

End to end record, John O'Groats, July 1910.

Triumph and Canoelet sidecar, February 1912. Mead and Deakin, makers of the sidecar, abroad.

Mr Pastela, Como, Italy, October 1911.

Minor adjustments, 1914.

Licence inspection, 1910.

Jack Marshall, TT winner for Triumph in 1908, poses on his race mount. Gordon Gibson stands alongside.

Aluminium single barrel.

The First Armoured Motor Battery, commanded by Sir John Willoughby. Photographed before heading overseas.

Corporal D Maple, 3½hp Triumph, after 14 months on active service.

A Triumph with Gloria munitions-carrier sidecar, April 1916.

Lieutenants Cecil S Burney (left) and Harris, back in England, engaged in training motorcyclists for despatch work at the front.

Corporal FN Foster, also 3½hp Triumph, also after 14 months on active service.

Corporal D Maple, 3½hp Triumph, after 14 months on active service.

Filling up 'somewhere' in the Near East, June 1915.

"HIS"

TRIUMPH

serving his country.   OUR triumph producing TRIUMPHS to assist in the triumph of the Empire.

TRIUMPH CYCLE Co., Ltd., COVENTRY.

TRIUMPH
STURMEY ARCHER 3 SPEED
COUNTERSHAFT GEAR.

In answering this advertisement it is desirable to mention "The Motor Cycle."   B13

Triumph Model Q Sports De Luxe, on top of the world, 1926.

Thanks to the sterling service of the Model H during the Great War, come peace time, then the Triumph brand was seen as an embodiment of all that was good with Britain. The Trusty Triumph had served its country with distinction and often without complaint, like so many young men. The people trusted the Triumph brand thanks in large part due to its war record.

Immediately after the war, the public was crying out for personal transport. So many men – and indeed women – who would never have left their village, never have travelled abroad, never have driven or ridden a motor vehicle, now had. Though the war had inflicted terrible suffering it had also changed the perceptions and aspirations of a generation and indeed generations to come. There was a feeling that life was for living and enjoying and motorcycles and the freedom they offered were an important part of that.

Triumph's initial post-Great War range was based upon a version of old faithful, the Model H. But there was soon a big shake-up – Claude Holbrook, Bettmann's old friend, joined as general manager and then later in the year, Schulte, who had done so much, was invited to resign, which he did with a £15,000 gratuity payment. Schulte and Bettmann had become increasingly far apart in their view of where the

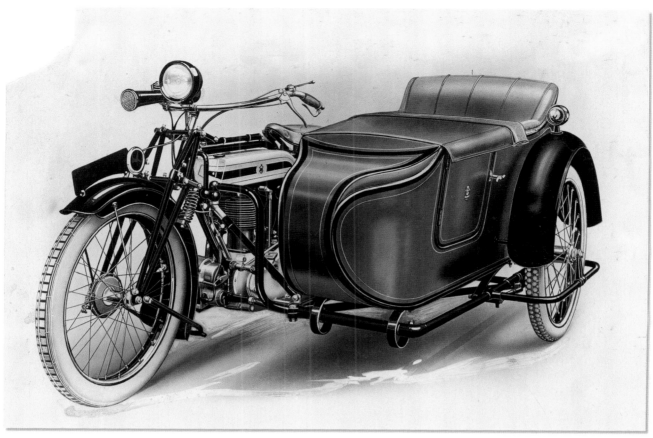

1925 Type SD13.

1920 SD.

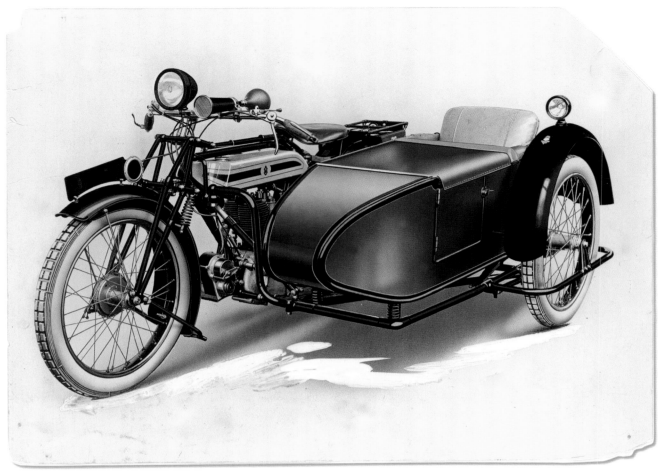

1924 Sports Combination.

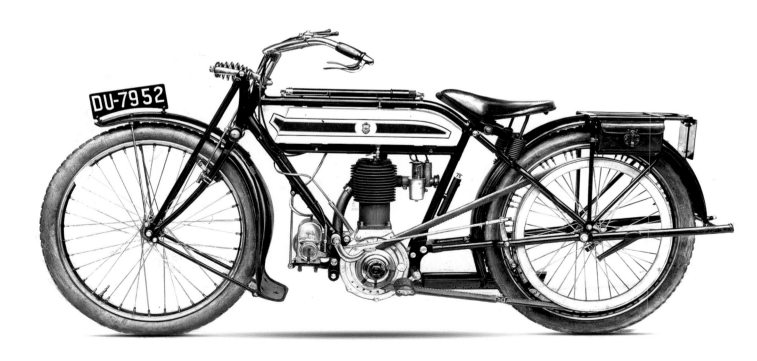

The Trusty Triumph – 1919 4hp.

company was going and with Bettmann employing his old ally Holbrook, and the majority shareholding enjoyed by Bettmann, one imagines that Schulte's position had become untenable.

Bettmann – and surely Holbrook – had the view that diversification was the future, while Schulte had been of the opinion it would be better to improve and continue to develop the core product, i.e. the motorcycles. But Bettmann's influence was greater and it was he who had the final say and Schulte who had to leave. The Triumph Motor Company was established in 1922 and the first four-wheeler was a 1400cc light saloon, built at the abandoned Hillman car plant in Coventry.

The motorcycle range had been developed in so much as that all chain drive had been adopted as had Triumph's own three-speed gearbox on the new 4hp SD (Sprung Drive). The company had also introduced a sportster – the four-valve Ricardo, which was basically an overhead valve sporting engine put into the standard rolling chassis. But the boom after WWI was nearly over and the world was heading for recession.

It was in this climate that Triumph launched the Model P, a 500cc machine which sold for the hard-to-believe figure of £42-17s-6d. There were teething problems, but 20,000 were shifted fairly rapidly and with the problems solved for the Mk.II version, at

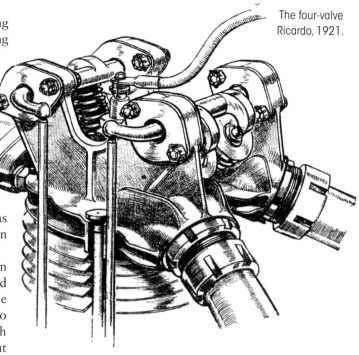

The four-valve Ricardo, 1921.

times production was topping 1000 units a week. The company was flying and by now the works – based in Priory Street – covered an area of 500,000 square feet and employed 3000 people. It was a massive operation but as the decade progressed, Triumph was experiencing the reality that even the biggest companies are not immune to world recession.

'Find this please.' Despatch riders' trial, September 1922.

Victor Horsman, Brooklands special.

Glasgow Team Trial, 1921, Mr Simons leaving the start.

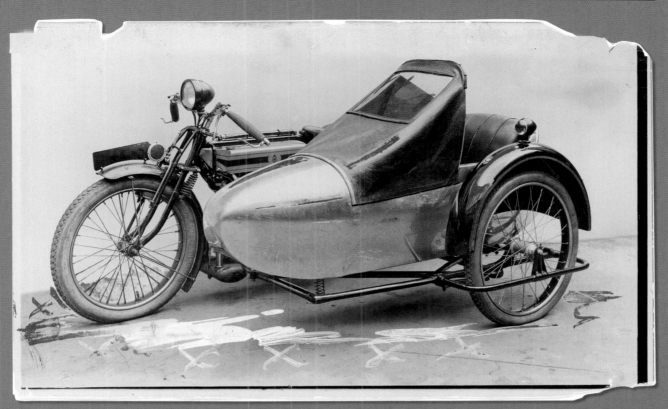

1922 Type R.

1925 (in Berlin).

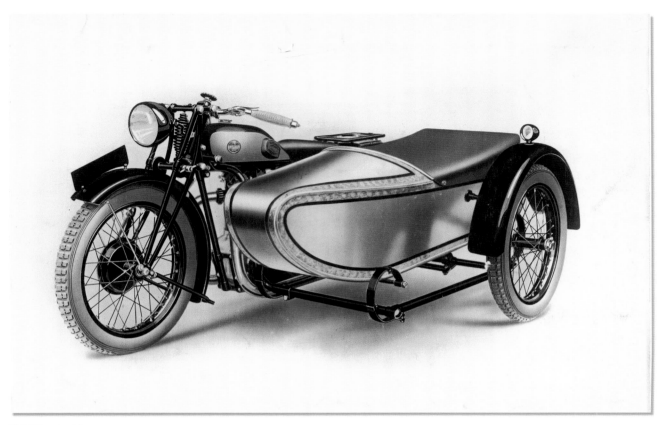

1929 Sports sidecar.

1928, with 'dicky' seat.

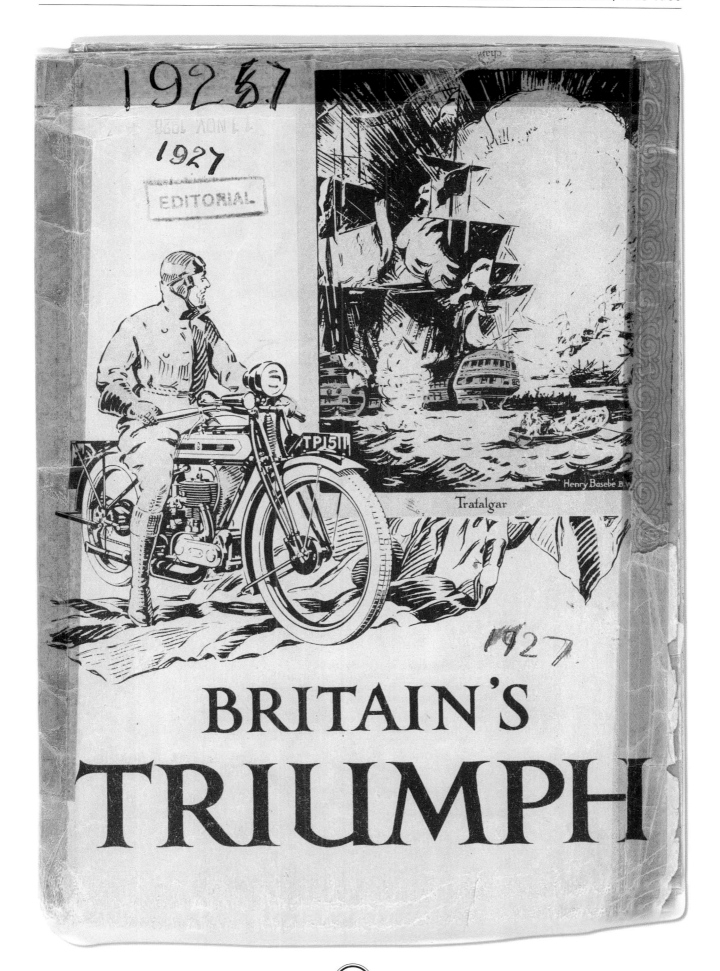

1928-model N De Luxe.

The 1923 346cc unit-construction model, with outside flywheel.

Bob Pollard, Crewkerne, Somerset, on his Ricardo, 1923.

1927-model 2.77hp Type W.

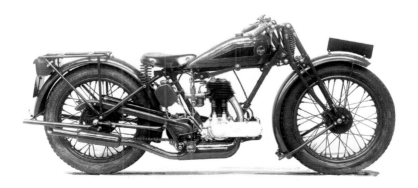

1928 LSD.

1925 MACHINES on the ROAD

The 494 c.c. TRIUMPH.

SPECIFICATION.

ENGINE: 84 × 89 mm. = 494 c.c., side-valve single cylinder.
LUBRICATION: Hand pump.
TRANSMISSION All chain.

GEAR BOX: Triumph three-speed, with clutch and kick-starter.
TYRES: Dunlop cord, 26 × 2½ in.

CARBURETTER: Triumph two-lever.
PRICE: £42 17s. 6d.

CAN a 500 c.c. single be marketed at under £45 and yet be a sound proposition?

How often has this question been debated since the Triumph Co. exploded its bombshell at Olympia.

With manufacturing costs these notes have little or no concern, but as regards roadworthiness of the latest Triumph our answer is an emphatic *Yes!* Not only is it a sound and businesslike proposition, but it is a pleasant machine to ride and remarkably tractable.

The new model has been designed as an all-purpose mount, so one does not expect to find an aluminium piston and super-compression. Nevertheless, with its cast-iron piston and moderate compression ratio of 4.5 to 1, the 494 c.c. Triumph has a good turn of speed, which, in the absence of accurate timing, we should judge to be in the neighbourhood of a 55 m.p.h. maximum.

Large valves (1⅛in. port diameter), a cylinder head designed to promote turbulence, and a crankshaft fitted with ball and roller bearings throughout, all help to produce a good performance, and—a point of some importance—the speed is accomplished without fuss on a gear of 5 to 1.

It would be untrue to state that the engine is vibrationless, for every single-cylinder engine is a compromise in the matter of balance. But the Triumph has no unpleasant period, and though there are smaller engines which give a relatively higher performance, the big single produces a comforting sensation of power quite unlike that given by a small unit running at high speed. Heavy flywheels and a moderate compression ratio, moreover, allow the engine to pull well at very low speeds.

Those who are too lazy to change into middle gear when crawling through thick traffic will experience a certain amount of snatch in the drive at very low speeds, but this can be eliminated by slightly easing the clutch.

This item, by the way, is a departure from Triumph practice, being of the dry plate type with floating fabric rings. It is entirely free from drag, smooth in action, and can be slipped to any required degree.

Mechanically, the engine and gear box are reasonably quiet, and though the power unit and silencer are quite new in design, the exhaust somehow retains the note characteristic of earlier Triumph models.

In low gear position the change speed lever lies alongside the tank, but in practice we found this to be no detriment to comfort, and, owing to the spring box included in the striking rod, the gears can be changed quietly and with certainty under all conditions. Further

II

B 21

910   THE MOTOR CYCLE   *DECEMBER 4th, 1924.*

1925 Machines on the Road.—

than this, the fact that the final chain is on the right-hand side should prove convenient for sidecar work.

A foot brake of the wedge pattern operating in a dummy belt rim is admirable in every respect. It is smooth and powerful, and those who have had experience with earlier Triumph models will appreciate the fact that the pedal is placed conveniently to the toe and does not necessitate the removal of the foot from the footrest.

The band brake on the front wheel was found excellent for holding the machine on an uphill grade while a restart was being made. Thus in a backward direction it holds admirably, but as a brake in the normal sense of the word it is poor, and one need have no fear of being thrown over the bars by a sudden application. Possibly it will improve with use.

Steering is well-nigh perfect, and the Triumph can be ridden "hands off" at any speed from about 12 m.p.h. upwards without a trace of wobble.

The machine was found to be steady in grease, and, even when inadvertently the rear wheel was locked during the descent of a greasy grass-surfaced hill of nearly 1 in 4, the Triumph slid forward in a straight line for many yards before swinging slightly out of line and coming to rest. This is an extreme test, and the machine behaved admirably under the circumstances.

A test of several thousand miles would be required before making a fair comparison between taper roller bearing hubs and well-designed cup and cone wheel bearings, so readers must be content with the remark that the roller equipped wheels on the Triumph run freely and without play, and no reason can be found why they should not last almost indefinitely without adjustment.

On hills the new Triumph is admirable. The machine tried out was quite new and had covered scarcely one hundred miles when it was first put at Edge Hill, yet, in spite of the fact that no effort was made to spare the engine—except for liberal oil injection—and that a very high average against a strong head wind had been maintained just previous to the ascent, the machine went more than halfway up the hill on top gear, and never showed

a symptom of distress. The remainder of the climb was child's play on middle gear, and, once well run in, the machine should accomplish the climb on top gear if circumstances be favourable, for grease on the lower bend handicapped the rider on this occasion.

Sunrising hill also proved an easy climb on middle gear, the machine travelling well round the hairpin before a change was necessary.

Two rough fuel consumption tests—over sixty miles in each case—showed that about 90 m.p.g. can be expected from the Triumph ridden solo. The first test was over a number of short journeys with much stopping, restarting, and traffic work. The second was over wet roads on a windy day, and included a fair amount of hill-climbing.

In spite of a very generous supply of oil, the engine kept remarkably clean, and only a trace of leakage was noticeable at one corner of the cylinder flange.

During two hundred and odd miles of road work only one minor trouble was experienced, due to a faulty plug, which caused bad starting from cold. A change of plug instantly cured the trouble, and thereafter the engine started easily and with certainty on every occasion.

To sum up the impressions gained on the road of this interesting machine, we may say that the latest Triumph is worthy of the high reputation of its sponsors. A critical eye may detect minor details on which money has been saved, but, in the things that matter, both material and workmanship appear to be of the best.

Sheet metal chain guards are not as refined as cast aluminium, and plain hand pump lubrication, though simple, safe, and effective, gives the rider rather too much to think about; but the engine, transmission, forks, wheel bearings, and tyres are of the best.

Less angular lines than those of earlier Triumphs characterise this latest addition to the range.

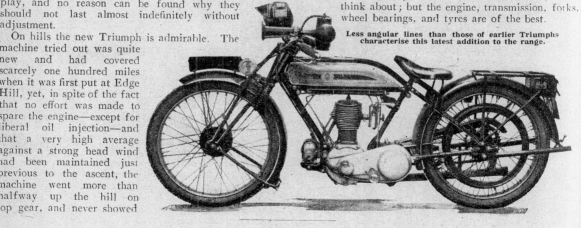

NO SPEED TEST FOR STOCK MACHINES.

IN the motoring notes of *The Field*, the omission of the speed test from the next A.C.U. 1,000 miles stock trial is commented upon. It will be noted that the opinion expressed agrees with that given in a leading article in *The Motor Cycle* of November 20th :—

As was noted in last week's *Field* the next 1,000 miles stock machine test to be organised by the A.C.U. will consist solely of a road trial, and there are, doubtless, many who will regret the elimination of the final speed test at Brooklands. . . . To our way of thinking, the Brooklands test imparted a spice of interest to the annual trial. It was an excellent means of weeding out the weaklings that had managed

to survive the road portion of the trial, and it set the final seal of durability on those mounts that covered the distance on the track in the prescribed time. . . . It must be remembered that the motor cycling public is very largely a sporting public, to whom speed makes a very definite appeal, and we believe a good deal of the interest that attached to the Six Days' events of the past will be lost as a result of the A.C.U. dropping the Brooklands test. The Union, to our mind, made an error when it confined the 1,000 miles event solely to stock models, thus depriving makers of the one big trial in the year which enabled them to try out adequately any new designs on which they were experimenting. The abolition of the speed test will still further lessen the interest and value of the "Six Days."

meantime, Page had departed – but next came perhaps the most significant appointment in Triumph's illustrious history, the recruitment of Edward Turner. Turner and Triumph were to become inextricably linked, their destinies woven together for all time.

Edward Turner was a bright young man, born in 1901. He had designed an overhead camshaft single and the famous Square Four, which was put into production by Ariel. It was Ariel that also benefitted from Turner's seemingly Midas touch when he introduced the Red Hunter range of 250, 350 and 500cc singles, with a bit of glitz and a catchy name about them. On his arrival at Triumph, Turner replicated his work at Ariel and Triumph's solid singles

were given a going over. What emerged was the Tiger 70, 80 and 90 line-up – handsome black, silver and chrome singles aimed squarely at the man who would have bought a Red Hunter the year before.

But more was to come – and what news it was. Probably the most important single step ever taken by Triumph was the decision to launch Edward Turner's Speed Twin on the public in 1938. It was a revelation, a sensation and set the template for the rest of Triumph's history. Finished in amaranth red and chrome, the Speed Twin was joined by the high-performance Tiger 100 in 1939 and Triumph had now moved smoothly back into position as one of Britain's leading motorcycle making companies.

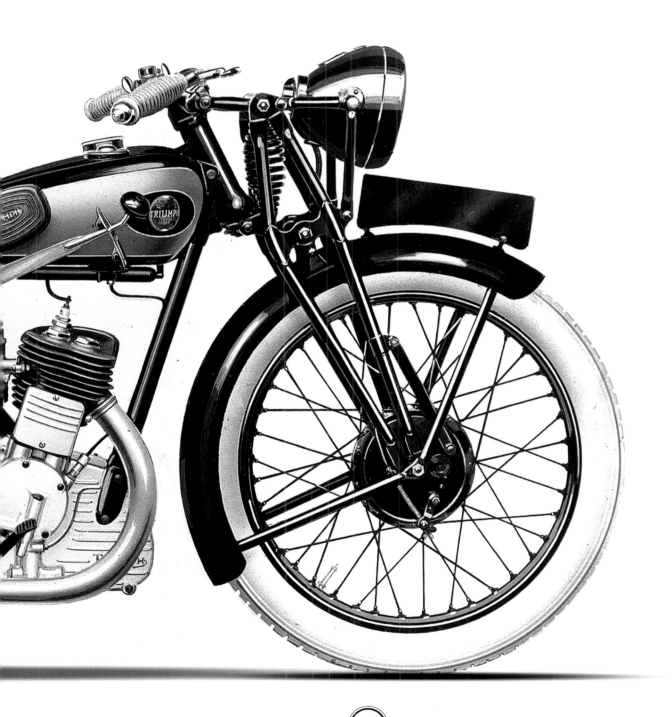

E Kendrew, Scarborough Motor Club Freak Hillclimb, July 1938.

The 1933 Ilkley Grand National; R Thompson (493cc Triumph) at Dob Park Splash.

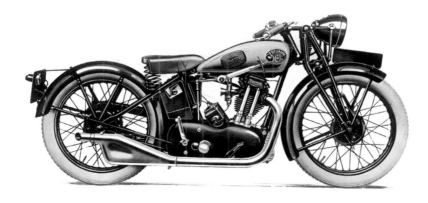

1933 250cc WA.

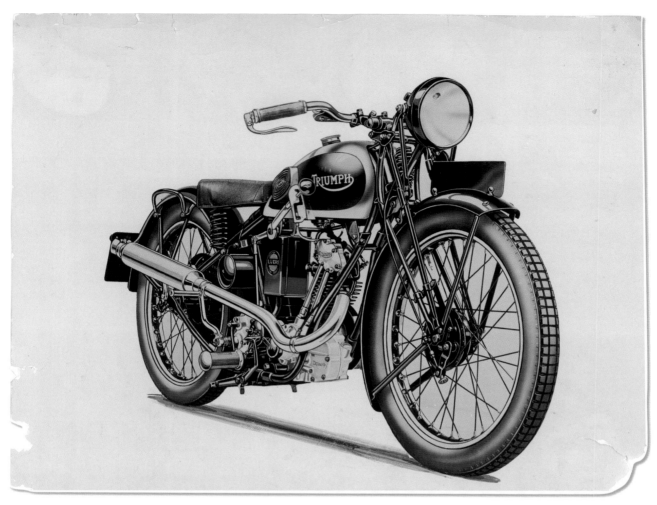

1935 150cc XO5/5.

1939 500cc 5S.

Freddie Clarke, March 1937, Triumph stock machine test.

October 12, 1933; 500 miles in 500 minutes, Brooklands, Surrey.

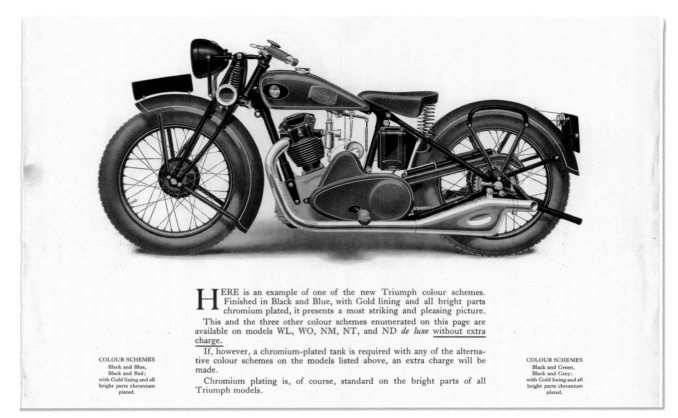

HERE is an example of one of the new Triumph colour schemes. Finished in Black and Blue, with Gold lining and all bright parts chromium plated, it presents a most striking and pleasing picture.

This and the three other colour schemes enumerated on this page are available on models WL, WO, NM, NT, and ND *de luxe* without extra charge.

If, however, a chromium-plated tank is required with any of the alternative colour schemes on the models listed above, an extra charge will be made.

Chromium plating is, of course, standard on the bright parts of all Triumph models.

COLOUR SCHEMES
Black and Blue,
Black and Red;
with Gold lining and all
bright parts chromium
plated.

COLOUR SCHEMES
Black and Green,
Black and Grey;
with Gold lining and all
bright parts chromium
plated.

Allan Jefferies, International Six Days Trial selection tests, July 1939.

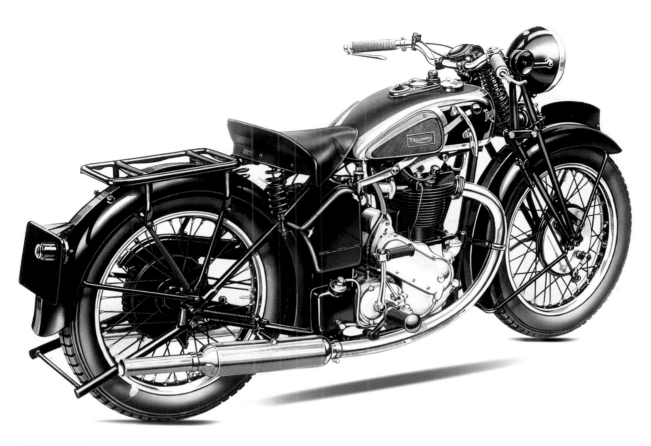

1935 Model 6/1.

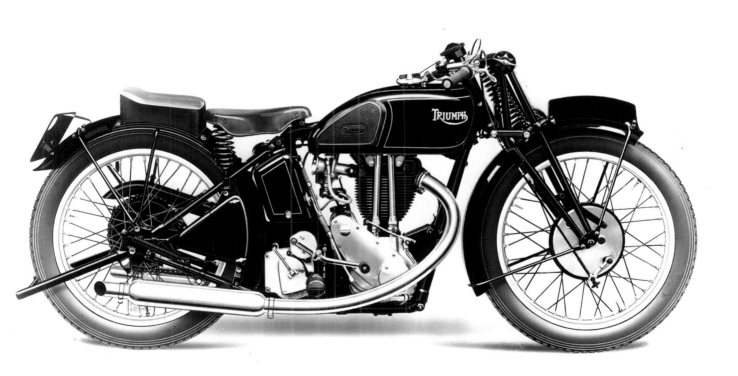

1936 Model 5/10;
price £80.

898　　　　　　　　　　MOTOR CYCLING　　　　　　October 20, 1937.

Road Tests of 1938 Models

THE 500 c.c. o.h.v. SPEED TWIN

TRIUMPH

A Fast and Flexible Multi

THE Speed Twin Triumph was undoubtedly one of the most outstanding models of the Show at Earls Court. Its 500 c.c. o.h.v. vertical twin engine attracted much favourable comment, and fast riders, whether they favoured single or multi-cylinder machines, could not fail to have been impressed by the high performance claimed for this newcomer. How fair these claims were is shown in the following report, which is the first description to be published of how a production edition performs on the road.

One of the first things to be noticed by the rider of a new machine is always the readiness with which it inspires confidence. In this respect the Triumph was good, and with one adjustment to the footrests the job fitted perfectly, the unusual shaped kneegrips giving an

almost exactly the same weight as a 500 c.c. single, with the weight distribution also practically identical.

The performance is excellent, and until very high revolutions are reached there is no vibration period at all; a normal cruising speed of 65-70 m.p.h. is very comfortable, at which rate of travel the whole machine runs very sweetly and quietly, with just a pleasing burble from the exhaust.

It would be difficult to imagine a twin of more compact design than the Speed Twin Triumph. The frame is finished in amaranth red to match the tank panels and the appearance, as a whole, is very smart.

excellent purchase on the tank. The handlebars are adjustable, but the position provided was correct for the rider and therefore no alteration was found necessary.

All handlebar controls are well laid out with the small exception of the dipper switch, which, as supplied, could not be operated without removing the left hand from the handlebar grip. The clutch and brake levers are nicely placed, providing a smooth action, and the twist-grip throttle is fitted with a clever device which allows easy movement but definitely prevents it closing of its own accord. As is well known, a self-closing throttle can be most annoying, particularly when signalling.

The gear-change and rear-brake operating pedals are just right; both can be operated without moving a foot from the footrests even when wearing heavy waders.

A useful indicator is fitted on the gear change to assist in finding neutral.

Perhaps the most interesting feature of this new model is the design of the twin engine. The cylinders, placed side by side, are so neatly laid out that it has the appearance of being a conventional two-port single. Apart from this, the weight problem has been very carefully considered, with the result that the machine is

General handling in town or country was above reproach and the riding position was comfortable and gave perfect control of the machine.

A14

ODEL

(Above) The Triumph proved its excellent road-holding over the bumpy concrete at Brooklands. (Left) The drive side of the power unit showing the disposition of the plugs and the faired-off chaincase. (Bottom, left) Top-gear performance on hills left nothing to be desired.

750 miles, worked out at 64 m.p.g. This included all types of going, such as pottering along country lanes, long-distance touring and traffic work. On a straight run from Kenilworth to Brooklands, 106 miles, covered at a high average speed, this figure improved to 68 m.p.g. Oil consumption was practically nil; after 500 miles it might have been possible to get $\frac{1}{2}$ pint into the tank, which gives a consumption of 8,000 m.p.g. Of course, the tank should be drained every 1,500 miles. The motor was fairly new and would no doubt use a little more after a few thousand miles.

Whilst on the subject of oil, leaks are practically non-existent, the only trace of leakage being from the joint between the rocker boxes and the cylinder heads. This does not take the form of liquid oil but a mere film which is shown up by road dirt adhering to it. The gearbox and oil-bath chaincase are just as clean, so that the best suit can be worn without any fear of oil stains.

Ease of Maintenance

Accessibility and ease of maintenance are matters of prime importance to the ordinary owner, most particularly in respect of the oil filters and chain adjustment. During the test it was not found necessary to adjust any part of the machine, which indicates the trouble-free running to be expected from a smooth but high-performance twin with fully enclosed valve gear.

Just to test accessibility, nevertheless, a little drill work was indulged in, starting with the valve adjustment. This is carried out at the valve end of the rockers, access being gained thereto by removing an inspection plug suitably situated over each of the rocker ends, and tightened up by means of a spanner.

The gearbox is pivoted, and a set screw gives an easy and positive means of tensioning the primary chain, and the rear wheel is moved by two setscrews, one located on each side of the rear forks.

The oil fillers for the gearbox, primary chain case and the engine oil tank are all so placed that refilling is an easy matter with any ordinary oil measure. The battery is carried on the near side of the saddle pillar, and, when the top cover has been removed by undoing one screw, can be filled up in situ.

Both the brakes are adjusted by finger screws, in the case of the rear brake at the rear end of the rod,

This may sound rather a high speed for cruising and tend to foster the idea that the performance lower down the range is not up to the same standard. On the contrary, any speed from 30 m.p.h. onwards was equally pleasant, and travelling normally, without consulting the speedometer, 45-50 m.p.h. was attained practically on the pilot jet. The top-gear performance runs from 10 m.p.h. to a cruising speed of 80 m.p.h.: these figures were taken with the rider wearing full touring kit (i.e., waders, trials coat and rucksack), and sitting up in a perfectly normal touring position.

The fuel and oil consumption were certainly not excessive, the petrol used, taken over the whole test of

A 15

900   MOTOR CYCLING   October 20, 1937.

Brief Specification of the 500 c.c. o.h.v. Speed-Twin Triumph

Engine: Vertical twin o.h.v. double high camshaft, 63 mm. bore by 80 mm. stroke = 497 c.c. Crankshaft mounted on ball bearings, with central flywheel. Forced-feed lubrication to big-ends and valve gear. All-gear drive to camshafts and Magdyno. Totally enclosed valves. Heavily webbed high-tensile aluminium alloy crankcase. H-section connecting rods in R.R. 56 Hiduminium alloy with split big-ends having steel caps lined with white-metal. Large-bore Amal carburetter.

Transmission: By four-speed foot-operated Triumph gearbox; ratios, 5.0, 6.0, 8.65 and 12.70 to 1. Primary chain enclosed in polished aluminium oil bath. Rear chain with guard.

Frame: Brazed full cradle of special alloy steel. Large diameter tapered front down tube. Taper tube girder forks with central compression spring and having dampers with finger adjustment on the lower bridge.

Wheels: Triumph wheels, with spokes of approximately equal length, fitted with Dunlop tyres. Tyre sections, 26 by 3.00 ribbed (front) and 26 by 3.50 Universal (rear).

Tanks: All-steel welded fuel tank with flush-mounted illuminated instrument panel carrying oil gauge, ammeter, switch and dash lamp. Capacity 3¼

gallons. Welded-steel oil tank with accessible filters and drain plug. Capacity ¾ gallon.

Dimensions: Saddle height, 27¾ ins.; wheelbase, 54 ins.; overall length, 84 ins.; overall width, 30 ins.; ground clearance, 5 ins.

Weight: 365 lb., fully equipped.

Price: £75, equipped with Lucas Magdyno lighting and electric horn.

Extra: Front-wheel-drive illuminated Smith trip speedometer supplied unless otherwise ordered at £2 15s. extra.

Makers: Triumph Engineering Co., Ltd., Coventry, England.

Tax: £2 5s. per annum.

ROAD TEST OF SPEED-TWIN TRIUMPH (Contd.)

and the front at the point where the Bowden cable meets the rod.

In order to test these points of maintenance it was necessary to make use of the tool kit provided, which was comprehensive and the quality good.

One of the essentials of any machine is good starting; in this respect the Speed Twin gets full marks. The machine was purposely left out for a night when the weather was a bit nippy, and the engine sprang to life at the first kick the next morning. Starting had been so good when the machine was given a normal stable that this test was thought necessary to prove what was considered to be an already established fact.

A tick-over on the pilot jet when dead cold was not obtainable, but after a very short run the twist grip could be turned right off and a pleasant tick-over was the result. Starting from cold there was slight piston slap, but when five or six miles had been covered this disappeared leaving a very high degree of mechanical silence; the gearbox was also extremely quiet on all the ratios.

Handling is a strong point of the new Triumph, and the model could be laid over on corners until the foot-rests prevented its going further. The type of bumps to be found on main roads did not seem to deter it from

following a straight and narrow path even without recourse to the steering damper.

In all honesty it must be said that such surfaces as the rough parts of Watling Street were more comfortable when the damper was just "nipped," when the speedometer was registering 75 m.p.h. or so, but at no time was there any real tendency to wobble with no damper action at all.

On loose sand and a portion of rough going the handling seemed good, whilst Birmingham tramlines and cobbles could be covered without any excitements provided reasonable care was exercised. The brakes were very powerful but quite smooth in action. On the particular model tested both the front and the rear wheel could be locked from 30 m.p.h. on dry concrete, and to bring the machine to rest from this speed only took 26 ft.

Taken all round the Triumph twin is one of the most pleasant machines to ride. Excellent flexibility, a genuinely high cruising speed, coupled with good road holding and comfort, make it an ideal mount for long-distance work at high average speeds, and it is equally suited for town work.

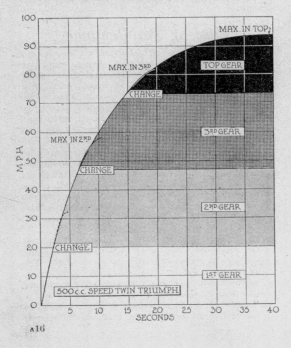

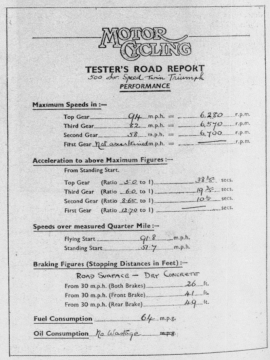

TESTER'S ROAD REPORT
500 o.h.v. Speed-Twin Triumph
PERFORMANCE

Maximum Speeds in :—

Top Gear	94 m.p.h. =	6,280	r.p.m.
Third Gear	82 m.p.h. =	6,570	r.p.m.
Second Gear	58 m.p.h. =	6,700	r.p.m.
First Gear	Not ascertained m.p.h. =		r.p.m.

Acceleration to above Maximum Figures :—

From Standing Start.

Top Gear (Ratio 5.0 to 1)	38½	secs.
Third Gear (Ratio 6.0 to 1)	19¾	secs.
Second Gear (Ratio 8.65 to 1)	10½	secs.
First Gear (Ratio 12.70 to 1)		secs.

Speeds over measured Quarter Mile :—

Flying Start	91.8	m.p.h.
Standing Start	51.7	m.p.h.

Braking Figures (Stopping Distances in Feet) :—

ROAD SURFACE — DRY CONCRETE

From 30 m.p.h. (Both Brakes)	26	ft.
From 30 m.p.h. (Front Brake)	41	ft.
From 30 m.p.h. (Rear Brake)	49	ft.

Fuel Consumption	64	m.p.g.
Oil Consumption	No Wastage	m.p.g.

A16

1938 Tiger 70.

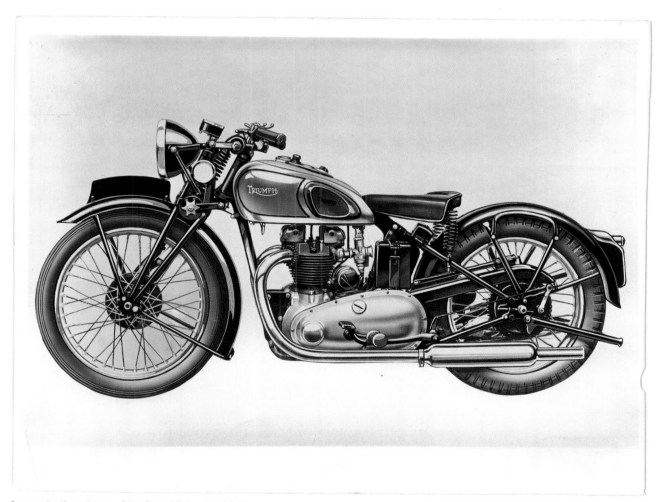

Pre-production picture of the Speed Twin, July 1937.

War service and war damage
1939-1945

33 MERIDEN 1943.

A new home; Meriden, 1943.

Bren gun
carrier, 1940.

At the outbreak of the Second World War, Triumph was riding the crest of a wave. The single cylinder Tigers were among the best and most attractive of their type on offer, while the twin cylinder Speed Twin and Tiger 100 had raised the bar in terms of sporting solos. Things could not be going better for the Coventry-based concern. So war came at a particularly bad time for the company. However, between 1938 and 1941, around 10,000 side-valve 3SWs were supplied to the military, replacing the 3S. In 1940, around 1500 5SWs were also supplied. The Second World War did have a huge, direct impact on Triumph when, in November 1940, the factory was heavily bombed. As well as destroying a lot of machines – a number of 3SWs plus the first batch of 50 of the 3TW model, a 350cc twin which Triumph had planned to produce in large numbers – much tooling, plans and spares were destroyed too, particularly for the 3TW. Mercifully – and incredibly – there was no loss of life in the Triumph works. But the raids left Triumph homeless. The bombing assault was of an unprecedented level. On the evening of November 14, 1940, more than 500 Luftwaffe bombers launched an attack on Coventry on a scale never before seen. The assault lasted over 10 hours and left much of the city devastated, with wave after wave of aircraft dropping bombs indiscriminately, destroying many buildings, including the city's 14th century cathedral.

Bombing began at 7.20pm and it wasn't until 6.15am that the all-clear was sounded. The raids on Coventry were termed 'legitimate' by the German high command, based on the fact that the city was home to so much heavy industry, making everything from bombs, to aeroplanes, to of course motorcycles, for the war effort. In fact, the RAF had bombed Munich – home to the Nazi party – on November 8, so many read the Coventry raid as a revenge attack. As the relentless November 14 attack on Coventry continued, so the resistance weakened. By 2am defences were ravaged, with anti-aircraft batteries running out of ammunition. Still they came though and it wasn't until 5am that there was any sign of let up. By the time it was all over, 554 people had been killed, 4330 homes destroyed and three quarters of the city's factories destroyed. It wasn't all Coventry had to endure though, as in April 1941 the city was again targeted, this time with raids of between six and eight hours.

After the November mauling, Triumph moved into an old foundry building at Warwick and set-to producing the 3HW model, based on the Tiger-80, while Triumph went about selecting a new site for the factory to be rebuilt on. A location at Meriden was secured and work commenced in July 1941, with some machinery in situ by March the next year – it was fully operational soon after. Triumph had a new home.

The despatch riders of the Women's Royal Naval Service (WRNS, or 'Wrens'), 1941.

July 1940; men from the second British Expeditionary Force (BEF), back after the evacuation from France.

An experimental Triumph 3SW Bren gun carrier, 1940.

The 1943 prototype 3TW 350cc twin. Graham Walker standing.

The 1943 prototype 3TW 350cc twin. Graham Walker standing.

With the end of the Second World War, it was a case of getting back to business. After six years of hard, brutal war, peace came about – but it wasn't now a case of 'an easy time for all.' There were still massive shortages and Britain, as a country, was in huge debt.

For 1946 Triumph had a range up and ready to go, which of course drew heavily on the pre-war models, the Tiger 100 and Speed Twin, but also featured a new 350cc twin – the 3T – plus a 350cc single, the 3H, which was basically a civilianised version of the 3HW. All the new models, though, differed in one important way from the pre-war examples in that all were fitted with telescopic forks.

Edward Turner, always confident that Britain would emerge from the hostilities victorious, had begun to think of how best to develop 'his' motorcycle manufacturer relatively early on during the Second World War. To that end, he'd decided that he needed to gain a strong presence in America and had been working on doing so during the war and as early as 1946 was exporting Triumphs across the Atlantic.

Another important happening for Triumph during the period was in September 1946, when Irishman Ernie Lyons won the Senior Manx GP on a Triumph twin. The machine, based upon a Tiger 100 but fitted with an all-alloy top end as used on wartime generator units, was developed in the works by

The Speed Twin, 1949.

Freddie Clarke, who had campaigned Triumphs pre-WWII and indeed held – and still holds – the 350cc and 750cc class lap records at Brooklands, set on a 350cc Triumph single and overbored 503cc Speed Twin. The legality of Lyons' machine was, in truth, somewhat dubious – the Manx was supposedly an 'amateur' event for privately owned machines and this one had been developed at the works and even sported a prototype sprung hub rear suspension set-up. But, whatever, Lyons, riding for the most part in driving rain, won at 76.74mph. A replica went on sale in 1947 and Don Crossley used a Grand Prix to win the 1948 Senior Manx GP.

In 1949, Edward Turner introduced two of his most famous developments – the headlamp nacelle and the Triumph Thunderbird. The nacelle went a long way to tidying up the handlebar area, introducing a flowing element and neatening what had always been a 'scruffy'

area on a motorcycle. Coupled with Triumph's neat, slim telescopic forks, it moved the machines into a whole new era from the 'cobbled together' look of pre-WWII girder forks/exposed springs/separate speedometer, into an altogether neater arrangement – which surely pleased Turner greatly.

The Thunderbird was a by-product of Turner's success in pushing Triumph in America. The brand had established a strong reputation Stateside, mainly on the back of the Tiger 100, but the cry had gone up for 'more cubes'. For a nation raised on a diet of big capacity V-twins, cubic capacity was all important and so though they loved the Tiger 100 and it outperformed the big sloggers they were used to (a good litl'un will beat a bad big 'un), the adapted adage 'a good litl'un will always get beaten by a good big 'un' meant the Americans wanted a good big 'un as well. And they got one, with the 'T-bird'.

The still-born Tiger 85, 1946.

Tiger 100s used by custom officials in the Russian zone of Austria, 1948.

Ernie Lyons winning the 1946 Manx Grand Prix.

1947 Tiger 100.

Grand Prix, 1949.

1950 dual-seat Speed Twin.

HRH Prince Bertil on the first Thunderbird in Sweden, December 13, 1949.

Triumph brochure, 1947.

Speed Twin engine, 1946.

272

THE MOTOR CYCLE

SEPTEMBER 29th, 1949.

Triumphs Introduce a 650 c.c. Twin!

First Three Production Models Average Over 92 m.p.h. at Montlhéry, then Do a Flying Lap at Over 100 m.p.h.

By GEORGE WILSON

The new 650 c.c. twin develops 34 b.h.p. at 6,000 r.p.m. The design is very similar to that of the Speed Twin engine

A 650 c.c. twin is introduced! A machine designed primarily for sustained high speeds on the vast, smooth highways of America, South Africa and Australia; with an engine developing 34 b.h.p. at 6,000 r.p.m.; and a total weight of little more than that of the famous 500 c.c. Speed Twin. Truly a mount to whet the interest of every enthusiast.

Last week, at the Montlhéry Autodrome near Paris, the first three production models, with full equipment, were subjected to the most severe standard machine test held post-war. The test was entirely successful. The three machines covered 500 miles at an average speed of 92.23, 92.48, and 92.33 m.p.h. respectively. Even taking into consideration stops for re-fuelling, change of riders, and, in one instance, changing a petrol tank which developed a leak, the respective averages were 90.30, 90.93, and 86.07 m.p.h. for the 500 miles. Even more astonishing, at the end of the 500

miles the machines did flying laps at 100.71, 100.71, and 101.78 m.p.h. respectively.

Riding the three were A. Scobie, J. L. Bayliss and S. B. Manns, of the Triumph staff; and Allan Jefferies and P. H. Alves. All arrangements were handled by H. G. Tyrell Smith and Ernie Nott. Harold Taylor, the famous sidecar driver, acted as official A.C.U. observer.

The test actually began a couple days before the Montlhéry "show," when the machines, fitted with panniers, set out from the works at Coventry. They were ridden through London en route to Folkestone, and, on landing in France, they were ridden again to Montlhéry. After the machines had been stripped of their panniers, they were given a preliminary run round the track, checked over, and the test embarked upon.

For the purpose of the test, several slight departures from production standard were made. For example, out of consideration of safety for the riders (and on Dunlop's advice) racing tyres were fitted. So that the riders could adopt the racing crouch comfortably, racing-type mudguard pads, small Trophy-model saddles, and fixed rearward footrests were used. Because of the position of the offside footrest, it was not, unfortunately, possible to use the kick-starter, so push starts were employed. Again because of the safety factor (an incandescent plug can easily lock an engine), K.L.G. racing plugs were fitted. Whereas the standard size main jet on the production job is 190, 210 jets were used in the test. Also, because the horn bracket on one of the

machines had fractured in practice, the horns were removed from all three machines. Extra strong clutch springs were fitted, and 25-tooth engine sprockets which will probably be standard for oversea, were used (24-tooth sprockets will be fitted on machines for the home market). Compression ratios were 7 to 1, as standard, and the fuel used was 72-octane Pool quality.

The Montlhéry track is concrete surfaced and very bumpy on the bottom curve. It measures 1.583 miles per lap and has steeply banked curves at each end. The track has immense width, so much so that when you take a machine round for the first time you hardly know where to point it! Because of the bump at the bottom, circling the track at speed is a job that is arduous in the extreme for both rider and machine.

A 95 m.p.h. Lap

On the morning of the day scheduled for the test, the track lay under a grey, cloudy sky dotted with blobs of blue. When the machines arrived, a capricious racing mount with a megaphone exhaust system was being patiently prepared for a record attempt. Work on the "freak" machine continued throughout the day; the job never performed satisfactorily, in marked contrast to the standard Triumphs, which from the word "go" gave of their best and kept on doing so quietly and without fuss!

Promptly at 9 a.m., Scobie set off on the No. 1 machine to complete a couple of warming-up laps before beginning the test proper. At 9.15 the actual test was on. Scobie was pushed off and got

Weight of the handsome new "Thunderbird" has been kept to a minimum. With spring hub fitted, the machine weighs 385 lb—little heavier than the 498 c.c. Speed Twin. The new Triumph tank finish will be noted

flat down to it right away. His first flying lap took him only 67s (85 m.p.h.). His next lap took 61, and the next 60s dead—a speed of 95 m.p.h. He was immediately given the signal to slow the pace!

At 9.21 a.m. Manns set off on No. 2 machine on his warming-up lap. Scobie had settled down to regular lappery at a speed of slightly over 93 m.p.h. Alves began his preliminary lap at twenty minutes to 10. The sun had now risen and was rapidly gaining strength. When Alves began serious batting, Scobie and Manns were lapping in easy, regular style and were separated by slightly less than the length of the straight. So quiet were the machines that they were inaudible when they were on the far side of the track. The zestful Scobie began to turn up the wick again and overhauled Manns. Again he was given the "S," and when he cut out the fireworks he was given the O.K.

The first hour passed. There was a certain tenseness at the pits. Would standard, equipped machines maintain this cracking speed? Nothing untoward occurred; each machine lapped with the utmost consistency.

"S" for Jefferies

When Scobie came in at the end of his tour, the tyres were cool and bore little signs of wear, though 66 laps had been covered at an average speed of 91.95 m.p.h. He reported that the most difficult part of the job was keeping the speed down! The engine was absolutely oil-tight; the only external oil seen was on the silencers—where it was being blown from the primary chaincase breather which is used on Triumphs to lubricate the rear chain. The pit stop was very brief; petrol and oil tanks were topped up. Bayliss set off, and Scobie rested.

No. 2 machine came in after the first hour looking as quondam as its sister job. It had covered 63 laps at an average speed of over 92 m.p.h.

Alves was lapping in 62.8s (about 91 m.p.h.), which was considered too slow and he was given the "F" sign.

Jefferies was flat on the tank and riding in too spirited a fashion. He was given "S."

So regularly did the three machines lap that watching them became monotonous. They circled hour after hour with clocklike precision. By then it seemed impossible that anything could possibly go wrong. But something did go wrong! Bayliss pulled into the pits at one o'clock on No. 3 machine with a split tank. Quickly the tank was removed and one from the spare machine fitted, the whole job taking 15 minutes. Bayliss set off again and settled down at once. The sun rose higher and higher above the clouds. The day became unbearably hot—and still the machines carried on. Stops for refuelling and change of riders came and went. If the machines were being overworked, they showed no sign of it.

At 2.20 p.m., No. 1 machine had completed five hours at an average speed, including stops, of 90.30 m.p.h. The monotony of watching this supreme example of sheer reliability was broken momentarily when Allan Jefferies came in on the bogey No. 3 machine to report that there was a high-pitched scream from the rear chain. All that was wrong, however, was that the bottom run of the rear chain guard was adrift. Quickly it was removed, and Jefferies set off again after a stop lasting about three minutes.

At the end of each machine's 500 miles there was still negligible external oil on the engines. Exhaust pipes, in fact, were only slightly discoloured near the port. Lights were still working on two of the machines, but had ceased to do so on the third; on that one also the ammeter needle had come away from its pivot. Rear chains were badly stretched; primary chains and tappets required no adjustment whatever.

When the machines had been checked and the rear chains adjusted, they each did a flying lap flat-out and achieved the speeds quoted earlier. I could not then resist having a whang on one of the machines, but because a free track was impatiently awaited by a French driver with a blown racing car, I

Allan Jefferies takes the "Thunderbird" round Montlhéry track at a speed around the century mark

got only three laps in before being flagged off.

The 650 c.c. Twin—to be called the Thunderbird, incidentally—is a man's machine if ever there was one. On my first circuit round the track I could not use full bore—this on a track four times as wide as the widest main road and with almost sheer banking on the curves —so phenomenal is the performance. On the second circuit I was clocking 100 m.p.h. on the straight past the pits, but again rolled the grip back when encountering the bump on the lower curve. Even on the third lap, I tended to shut off slightly, although I was getting the feel of things with each tour.

The engine felt to be working no harder at 100 m.p.h. than my own Speed Twin engine is at 75-80. Acceleration is far and away superior to that of any five-hundred and is definitely of the racer variety. Low-speed torque was not so good as I had expected,

The three Triumphs, after completing the 500 miles, covered a flying lap. Riders are, left to right, S. B. Manns, L. J. Bayliss, and A. Scobie

274   THE MOTOR CYCLE   SEPTEMBER 29th, 1949

TRIUMPHS INTRODUCE
—A 650 c.c. TWIN—

but, of course, with the machine's 25-tooth engine sprocket, the gearing was higher than that to which I am accustomed.

What of the new model's technical features? The Thunderbird design is based on that of the long-established Speed Twin—forerunner of every other vertical-twin in production to-day. Bore and stroke of the engine are 71×82mm, as against 63×80mm for the five-hundred. Graphs showing the power curves of the new engine and the Speed Twin reveal that the Thunderbird engine develops the same b.h.p. at 4,000 r.p.m. as the Speed Twin does at 6,000. At 6,000 r.p.m., the 650 c.c. engine is producing 34 b.h.p. on a 7 to 1 compression ratio: 7½ more h.p. than the Speed Twin at similar engine speed.

However, the full advantage of the larger capacity engine is not to be found in sheer h.p. at high r.p.m. alone. The power curve is "flat," and the torque at low revolutions per minute—in fact, at all revs.—is vastly superior to that of the Speed Twin.

Stronger Con-rods

With true Triumph ingenuity the weight has been kept to a bare minimum. Indeed, the difference in weight between the Thunderbird and the Speed Twin is no more than a pound or two. The approximate weight is 365lb or, with the spring hub, which is an optional fitting, 385lb. Thus we have a fully equipped six-fifty with rear-springing delivering 34 b.h.p. and tipping the scales at 385lb; a 650 c.c. retaining all the handling attributes of a British five-hundred and possessing the high, effortless cruising speed of the 700lb or so machines popular in the U.S.

Though inertia stresses in the new engine are likely to be less than those of the 500 c.c. twin, power for power—as given power is achieved at lower revs—stronger connecting rods are fitted.

These are light-alloy, H-section stampings in RR56, and are almost identical in design with the rods used in the Grand Prix engines. The lower half of the big end eye is a white-metal-lined steel forging, and the unit is held together by a pair of 100-ton tensile strength nickel-chrome big-end bolts. In journal diameter and proportion the crankshaft is of the same dimensions as that of the five-hundreds, but, of course, the throw is increased by 1mm to give the 82mm stroke.

The cylinder head and barrel are almost identical in appearance with those of the Speed Twin. In fact, a casual glance reveals virtually no difference.

Sufficient Power

Efficient combustion chamber design is cleverly achieved. Valve geometry is not decided, as is usual, by the machined hemispheres of the combustion chambers. Instead, each valve has its own supplementary hemisphere machined about the valve seat. The advantage of this is increased compression ratio without resort to an exaggerated dome on the piston. Thus the weight of the piston is kept down and an efficient combustion chamber is achieved.

A Tiger "100"-type Amal carburettor with a choke diameter of 1in is fitted. The induction manifold in the head conforms to Speed Twin practice except that it has larger-cored passages. It was explained by Mr. Edward Turner that the fitting of an even larger carburettor gives increased top-end power, but that there is so much power available that this is not only unnecessary, but undesirable! Valves measure 1 7/16in across the seat—an increase of 1/16in over those of the Speed Twin. Rockers, push-rods, tappets and cams are identical with those of the Speed Twin, and there is no deviation from Speed Twin valve or ignition timing.

Originally, on the Speed Twin, rocker-gear oil draining was by means of external pipes which led the oil down to the push-rod tubes. In later models these oil drains were drilled in the cylin-

der, thus obviating the need for external oil pipes. The original draining scheme has been reverted to in the 650 c.c. engine since, with the larger bores, there is insufficient metal to accommodate drilled oilways.

Apart from these differences, the remainder of the engine is identical with that of the Speed Twin. Six-fifty and five-hundred timing gear is interchangeable, and the crankcases are virtually identical as regards appearance. The oil-pump of the 650 c.c. engine, however, has increased capacity, circulating some 25 per cent more oil.

In order to cope with increased b.h.p., the transmission has been slightly modified. An extra plate has been added to the clutch, making a total of five plates. The gear box itself has been redesigned and opportunity has been taken in the redesigning to provide easier engagement from 1st to 2nd and from 2nd to 3rd gears. This has been achieved by re-

A cutaway illustration of the ingenious Triumph spring hub, which is an optional extra on the Thunderbird

lieving alternate dogs. The 24-T. sprocket gives top, 4.57; third, 5.46; second, 7.75; bottom, 11.2 to 1. A further change in the gear box is the provision for an integral speedometer drive. The cable now emerges horizontally from the gear box on the timing side of the machine, and allows the cable to pass up to the speedometer head in an easy sweep.

Triumphs have decided, on the score of reliability, not to chromium-plate tanks in future. It has been found, as was pointed out in a Leader in *The Motor Cycle*, that particularly in the case of machines sent oversea, trouble has been experienced with rust, the deposit of which is encouraged by the combination of the plating process and the consequent sea-crossing. It has also been ascertained that chromium plating tends to weaken the welded seams. The Thunderbird tank is therefore finished in an attractive shade of grey-blue, and there is a tank motif in the form of a chromium-plated band on which is mounted the badge.

Steering geometry, frame proportion, wheelbase, brakes, saddle height, and riding position are identical with those of the Speed Twin. The handlebar nacelle is, of course, being retained. Tank-top parcel grids, because of their popularity, have been standardized on Thunderbird models; the speedometer, also, is included in the purchase price.

What of a production date? The first of the new models should be leaving the factory during the second week in October. Although the initial production will go oversea, it is anticipated that a good proportion will be made available for riders at home before Christmas. The price is £153, plus Purchase Tax (in Great Britain only), £41 6s 3d, making a total of £194 6s 3d, without spring hub, but including speedometer and parcel grid. The spring hub costs £16 (plus P.T. £4 6s 5d). The makers are the Triumph Engineering Co., Ltd., Meriden Works, Allesley, Nr. Coventry, England.

Good show : Mr. Edward Turner, managing director, Triumphs, congratulates all concerned immediately after the arduous test

Chapter 7
On top of the world
1951-1960

Triumph entered the 1950s in a position of power. In Edward Turner, the company possessed the man most in the motorcycle industry would like running their company, a man seemingly with the happy ability to turn everything he touched to gold. One of the products that was the result of Turner's said Midas touch was the 649cc Thunderbird, which at the beginning of the 1950s, was arguably the most desirable of motorcycles out there, certainly for the man in the street. And the T-Bird was backed up by a range that was packed full of quality, from the friendly 350cc 3T, to the sporting Tiger 100, the trusty Speed Twin and the competition-biased Trophy and Grand Prix. Life was, indeed, good at Meriden.

And it carried on in a similar vein through the early 50s. Though some mumbled that Turner's sprung hub wasn't up to much, it didn't stop Triumphs selling well indeed. But Turner was aware that his company

didn't have an entry level machine, one to tempt the youngsters and 'hook' them onto the Triumph, so that they'd be buyers for life. It was something he attempted to address with the Terrier, a 150cc single which had styling aping the bigger models in the range. It was launched in November 1952 and it and its developments were to spawn quite a dynasty themselves.

Soon after the Terrier barked into the sunlight, in 1954 the Tiger 110 roared into being. Those insatiable, capacity-hungry Americans had been briefly sated by the Thunderbird but now they wanted more! So, Turner responded with the Tiger 110 (Ton-ten) which was based upon the T-Bird, but boasted bigger valves and ports, higher compression pistons, different camshafts – and an all-new swinging arm frame.

In 1953 a small-budget film, *The Wild One*, loosely based around the happenings at Hollister in 1947, was

74

When Mr and Mrs WK Nelson of Hollywood arrived at Triumph to take delivery of a Thunderbird and Swallow Jet 80 sidecar outfit, they had no previous experience of motorcycling. After driving instructions on the work's sports field, the couple left for a three-month-long continental trip. *The Motor Cycle*, June 1952.

made. The central character of the film was disaffected youth Johnny, played by Marlon Brando. *The Wild One* – which shocked audiences in its day – placed Johnny on a Thunderbird and despite legend saying Triumph apparently tried to distance themselves from the movie, an iconic image was established and Triumph's name boosted. It was no coincidence that another icon of 50s 'disaffected youth', James Dean, rode a Triumph.

The swinging arm frames spread through the range and then on September 6, 1956, there was an important happening at Bonneville Salt Flats, when Johnny Allen achieved a speed of 214mph with his fully streamlined, tuned Triumph twin. It was to prove an important event in the history of Triumph.

Another big event was the launch of the first unit-construction (engine and gearbox in unit) twin, a cute 350cc model named the 3TA Twenty-One. It was a big step and arguably the most significant event since launch in the history of Triumph twins – the progressing from a separate engine and gearbox to all unit set up. This was to be followed by a 'unit' Speed Twin a year later though the 'big bikes' (the 650s) saw out the 50s as pre-units.

But, in retrospect, probably the biggest event of the period for Triumph was the first appearance in its line-up of a model with a name that will forever be synonymous with – the Bonneville (thanks for the name, Johnny A!). Launched for the 1959 season, the twin-carb sportster – again aimed squarely at those power-mad Americans – would go on to be well known...

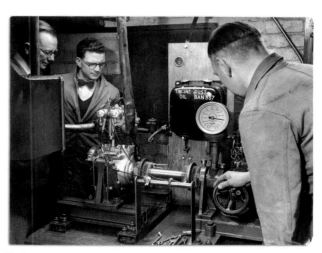

Engine testing, 1953.

1952 ISDT machine.

On the buses, 1957.

Whittaker's Cub-based racer, Mallory Park, March 1958.

Have Triumph, will travel, 1955.

Six Americans at Stratford-on-Avon in July 1952, on their Thunderbirds.

The Geneva show, 1958.

Californian tuner Joe Dudek with his 650cc Triumph, August 1958.

Travelling marshals at the TT, 1955.

TRIUMPH
SPEED TWIN
500 cc
Patent Nos. 475860, 474963, 482024

The Triumph Speed Twin in its all amaranth red finish is possibly the best known motorcycle in the world today. It was the first of all the modern vertical twins and established the overwhelming popularity of this type of engine—designed, developed and proved entirely by Triumph. Chosen by over 150 police and similar bodies for its complete reliability and silent performance. *Full Specification on pages 10/11.*

5

Catching up with the news, June 1954.

President Eisenhower and Prime Minister Macmillan, with Triumph escort, London airport, 1959.

Tiger 100, 1953.

Member of North London branch of the Triumph Owners Club, instructing at RAC/ACU training course.

German Klavs Bornagh on his T110 in South Australia, 1957. Extreme left is CM Moyse, of Lenroe Motorcycles, the other rider is Helmut Schon (Royal Enfield).

John Giles, winner Bramley scramble, April 1957.

Either ends of the range – Bonnevilles and Cubs for export, 1959 models.

Crowded Brixham harbour, November 1955.

T110s delivered to the Swedish police. The riders attended a course at the Army Motor School, Strängnäs.

Jack Dale, clad in bathing trunks, on Bus Schaller's Thunderbird, Bonneville, 1954.

Mrs Hazel Rochard of Harringay prepares to ride into Brussels, 1959.

Miss Jean 'Montana' Baker, a school teacher from Great Falls, Montana, holds an award given to her at the races at Belknap, New Hampshire, for riding the greatest distance to the event. *The Motor Cycle*, November 1953.

Triumph Owners Club rally, at Meriden, 1958. Riders (from left) K Wakefield, E Dyson, BC Barrow and G Cooke.

Roy Peplow at Hawk's Nest, in Clayton, Derbyshire, on the Tiger Cub, in 1958.

The 1958 range on display in Daytona.

The new Triumph Terrier, 1953.

Johnny Allen (centre) with his bullet-shaped streamliner, on the Bonneville Salt Flats, September 1959. Others are Stormy Mangham (left) and Pete Dalio.

Tiger Cub under critical gazes, November 1955.

Testing out a Tiger Cub, 1957.

Pilots with their pride of Tigresses in front of a Supermarine Scimitar jet fighter, at Farnborough Air Show.

Ted Young (ETY Triumph) with passenger DC Young, Brands Hatch, May 1958.

Brave new era; publicity picture for the unit 'Twenty-One,' 1957.

1951 Senior Clubman's TT, Ivan Wickstead races to second.

794   MOTOR CYCLING   *October 23, 1958*

Next Year's Triumphs

A New, Lower-priced " Speed Twin " and a " Bonneville 120 " Feature in the Nine-model Meriden Range, Practical Road Impressions of Which Appear on Pages 804-5 of This Issue

Latest—and fiercest—specimen of the genus tiger, the T120 " Bonneville 120 " is a road-going machine with a maximum speed nearly 20 m.p.h. over " the ton." Above is the manufacturers' output curve for the 46 b.h.p. engine. The close-up below shows the splayed-port cylinder head and twin special Amal carburetters, with remote rubber-mounted float bowl.

RELINQUISHING the TR5 " Trophy " model, but introducing a new sports roadster in the form of the 650 c.c. " Bonneville 120," Triumphs maintain a range totalling nine machines for 1959. Each is a series model; this is to say, it is already well established basically, but subject to periodic development in the light of changing needs and this process is responsible for the inclusion now in the 1959 range of a " 500 " with unit-construction characteristics of the 350 c.c. Model " Twenty-one." It becomes a brand-new version of the " Speed Twin " and at £245 15s. 2d. (including tax) is £7 9s. 9d. cheaper than its predecessor.

Sub-division of the range under three headings simplifies grouping in which " A " models are the lightweight T20 and T20C " Tiger Cubs "; " B "-range machines are the " 500s " and " 650s," for which separate engine and gearbox assemblies are retained; while the " C " machines are the unit-construction " Twenty-one," now listed as the 3TA and the new " Speed Twin," now called the 5TA. Detail changes and colour modifications apply to most machines in the old range.

Improvements to the " A " category include, outstandingly, a neat centre fairing, the panels being quickly detachable for maintenance purposes. And there is technical merit in the adoption of a new cylinder barrel with more substantial finning and cored tunnels for the through studs. A Zenith carburetter, a mid-1958 " Tiger Cub " modification, too, is retained and incorporates

A10

a new air cleaner mounted at the carburetter bell mouth instead of being built in. A new petrol tank of more substantial appearance, though no greater in capacity, is a T20 feature, the T20C competition model continuing with the narrower tank. Twin seals at the gearbox final driveshaft are now used for oil retention and the exclusion of dirt and water and for the " Competition Cub " provision has been made for the fitting, if necessary, of a larger gearbox final-drive sprocket. Colour finish is unchanged, namely, silver-grey and black with black frames.

The bulk of the range comes into the " B " category, the group being headed by the T100 " Tiger 100," which continues as before save for the alternative two-tone finish in which the petrol tank now carries a dominating white upper panel, the lower half being finished black—a reversal of last year's arrangement. Standard finish is silver-grey and black, a *décor* matching the " all-alloy " engine. Salient " B " specification features are separate engine and gearbox units; Triumph " Slickshift " automatic clutch operation and separate dynamo and magneto units. A single Amal 376/35 carburetter is standard but the T100 is still to be available with a splay-type two-port inlet light-alloy cylinder head and twin Amal carburetters.

Changed least of all for next year, the

T110 " Tiger 110 " is a sports roadster with cast-iron cylinder and light-alloy head assemblies and a capacity of 649 c.c. Colour finish is identical with that for the 498 c.c. " Tiger 100 " and the reversal of ivory/black tank panels also applies to the optional two-tones.

High-compression pistons and special camshafts producing some 40 b.h.p. make the T110 engine specification acceptable for the sports TR6 " Trophy." This model shares with four other " B " range machines the separate dynamo and magneto arrangement, but there is a suggestion of bare functionalism in the upswept " Siamesed " exhaust pipes on the TR6: the " Twinseat " is slimmer, more business-like; high-clearance mudguards are fitted and the front forks are protectively gaitered at the telescoping edges. Developed under International Six Days conditions, the " Trophy " model has well-established endurance qualities. Triumph " Trophy " machines went to Germany for the I.S.D.T. last month finished in ivory and Aztec red, a colour combination pre-

viously available for U.S.A. customers only, but now adopted as standard.

Continuing with an " all-iron " engine, the 1959 6T " Thunderbird " loses its S.U. carburetter in favour of an Amal instrument and embodies the latest Lucas RM15 alternator, a smaller assembly than that used hitherto, but one with equivalent electrical output. Rectifier, battery and H.T. coil equipment give the 6T full A.C./D.C. elec-

ville 120." Cast-iron barrel and splay-inlet light-alloy head carrying twin $1\frac{1}{16}$-in.-choke special Amal carburetters, with a remote rubber-mounted float bowl, are standard: maximum performance derives from a " Tiger 110 " E3325 exhaust cam form in conjunction with an E3134 inlet camshaft. Standard valves and high-compression pistons (8.5 : 1) produce the 46 b.h.p. power output necessary for near 120-m.p.h. road speeds.

Details of the original conversion parts, and their fitting, are set out in Triumph's " Technical Bulletin No. 2," but an important aspect of the complete production machine is selective assembly and bench-testing. Each " Bonneville 120 " conforms

The T20 "Tiger Cub" now appears with a neat central fairing formed of quickly detachable panels, a new cylinder barrel with improved finning, a restyled petrol tank and a number of detail modifications.

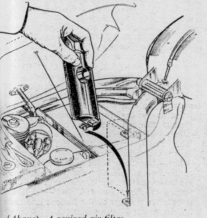

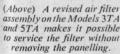

(Above) A revised air filter assembly on the Models 3TA and 5TA makes it possible to service the filter without removing the panelling.

(Right) Completely new model is the 5TA "Speed Twin," virtually a 500 c.c. version of the "Twenty-One," with the rear enclosure, unit-construction engine and excellent steering geometry of the 350 c.c. machine. With a 69 mm. bore, the capacity is 489 c.c.

trical character in which separate dynamo and magneto units of the conventional type play no part. One of the early post-war developments in 650 c.c. vertical twin design, the " Thunderbird," continues but with a new, sombre, but dignified charcoal-grey and black.

In recent years a comprehensive conversion kit has made possible increased use of the high-performance potential latent in the 500 c.c. and 650 c.c. engines—particularly the T110—and it is the application of such parts which largely results in the existence now of a new " 650 " listed as the " Bonne-

to a standard, the required output being shown by the graph on page 794. This output performance is obtained with the cams and carburetters above-mentioned and $1\frac{1}{2}$-in.-diameter exhaust pipes. " Tiger 110 " general specification, less " Slickshift," applies to the new " Bonneville 120," which is finished in pearl-grey, tangerine and black.

New for all " B "-range models is a one-piece forged crankshaft, providing a sturdy " bottom-half " commensurate with the ever-increasing performance demands. For the same reason T120, T110 and TR6 oil tanks embody a froth tower in the top panel designed to prevent aeration under sustained high-speed running conditions. Better front-brake geometry accrues from the use of a new cam lever positioned to give maximum leverage over a longer period of use. A modified piston skirt form, reducing

A11

1967 Tiger 100.

Malcolm Uphill, winner 1969 Production TT, at an average speed of 99.99mph.

British boxer Henry Cooper – with brother George on pillion – aboard a 1962 T120.

T110 on patrol, late 1961.

Bond girl Mollie Peters (*Thunderball*) with a T10 scooter.

498

MOTOR CYCLE 25 OCTOBER 1962

ONE-PIECE SIX-FIFTIES

New Frame for the Bigger Triumphs: Sports Three-fifty

MAYBE you are too young to remember the Tiger 90; but Dad knew it well, as a hot-stuff five-hundred of the 1930s. Tiger, from the way it ate up the miles; 90, the potential maximum. Well, the name is back in the Triumph list for 1963. Same derivation, of course, except this time the model is a 349 c.c. twin, a high-performance middleweight with a specification akin to that of the well loved Tiger 100.

There's even bigger news from Meriden, for the whole six-fifty group is revised, to incorporate unit-construction of engine and gear box in a new frame design of great lateral rigidity. A novel clutch operating mechanism, too, and a three-vane shock absorber to smooth out the drive still further.

But let's begin with those boisterous little 199 c.c. Cubs—four in all: the Tiger Cub roadster, Cub Sports, and trials and scrambles works replicas. There's a much tidier engine-gear unit for the latest Tiger Cub and Cub Sports, for gone is the distributor head which used to poke up through the top face of the crankcase, abaft the cylinder barrel.

Instead, the contact-breaker assembly is housed in a swelling in the timing cover—out of the way, yet easy to reach.

A welcome improvement is the provision of an oil-tank drain plug. Other new features include the latest Lucas miniature rectifier (used throughout the Triumph range) operated by silicon crystals, attractively finned rocker-box covers, new anti-vibration mountings within the speedometer head—and gear-position indicator.

Previous Cubs had a gear indicator on top of the head-lamp nacelle, but that is replaced by a plunger, bearing an engraved scale, which rises through the top face of the gear box after the style of a tyre-pressure gauge.

349 c.c. Tiger 90—1963 version

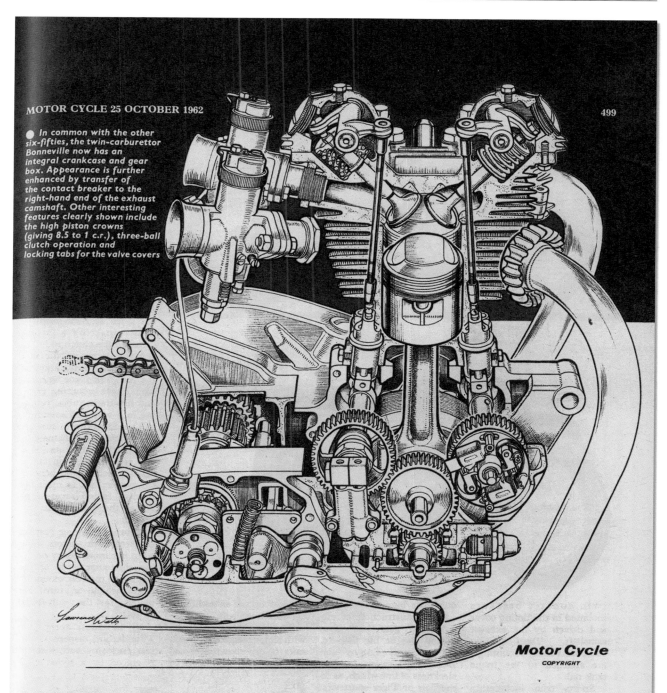

MOTOR CYCLE 25 OCTOBER 1962

499

● *In common with the other six-fifties, the twin-carburettor Bonneville now has an integral crankcase and gear box. Appearance is further enhanced by transfer of the contact breaker to the right-hand end of the exhaust camshaft. Other interesting features clearly shown include the high piston crowns (giving 8.5 to 1 c.r.), three-ball clutch operation and locking tabs for the valve covers*

Motor Cycle
COPYRIGHT

There is a general cleaning-up of the nacelle itself, which now carries separate lighting and ignition switches.

At extra cost, the Sports Cub can be fitted with a rev-meter, in which case the drive is taken from behind the cylinder.

Exact copies of the models used by the factory's own teamsters, the trials and scrambles Cubs continue without major change. Col-

ours of the Sports Cub and the two competition specials are burgundy and silver; the standard Tiger Cub has a fuel tank in flame and silver and flame-tinted oil tank and tool-box lid.

Four unit-construction twins make up Group C, the 490 c.c. Speed Twin and Tiger 100, and the 349 c.c. Twenty One and Tiger 90.

Improvements common to all include grease-retaining seals inboard of the wheel

bearings, a three-vane clutch shock absorber with greater movement than before (and, hence, a smoother action), and knurled-edge rocker caps secured by a spring-blade locking device.

The long-skirt rear enclosure is retained for the two tourers (Speed Twin and Twenty One) and the exhaust system reverts to twin pipes and silencers. Cherry red is the finish of the five-hundred, but as an alterna-

tive to shell-blue sheen the three-fifty is also available in silver bronze.

This year's debutante is, of course, the Tiger 90, with a power unit based on that of the Twenty One but with larger-diameter inlet valves, a sports camshaft, 9 to 1 compression ratio and a larger-bore carburettor ($\frac{15}{16}$in choke as against $\frac{25}{32}$in).

Specification is similar to that of the Tiger 100, and both sports mounts now have

500

349 c.c. Twenty One

MOTOR CYCLE 25 OCTOBER 1962

eliminating low-speed rattle, a thrust washer is now located inboard of the clutch sprocket, while the load is taken directly on the sprocket face.

Actuating mechanism, at the right-hand end of the clutch thrust rod, comprises a pair of steel pressings (one secured to the gear-box cover, the other rotated by operation of the clutch cable) between which are three steel balls seated in indents. As the inner pressing is rotated, so the balls ride up the sides of their seatings, thus imparting a lateral thrust to the clutch rod.

Main feature of the new frame is the integration of the rear-fork pivot with the engine rear mounting plates and sub-frame tubes, resulting in a very stiff assembly.

The front-down tube is really hefty ($1\frac{5}{8}$in-diameter $\times$ 12-gauge!) and to its lower end are welded twin cradle tubes which extend beneath the power unit to meet the massive forged cross-member at the base of the seat tube.

Another forging carries the rear-fork pivots, and whip is eliminated by securing the outer ends of the forging to the rear mounting plates which, in turn, are bolted to the sub-frame struts.

In its latest form, the Thunderbird dispenses with rear enclosure and, instead, is graced by a styled mid-

649 c.c. Thunderbird

twin contact breakers mounted in the timing cover and driven by the exhaust camshaft. Twin ignition coils, on rubber mountings, are attached to the frame tank rail.

Sports trim includes a chromium-plated headlamp carried on brackets from the front-fork shrouds, frame midriff enclosure (with separate ignition and lighting switches mounted on the left-side panel) and a siamesed exhaust system with new-type resonator silencer designed for minimum power loss with maximum efficiency.

Finish of the Tiger 90 is a startling Alaskan white, with gold and black lining. Regal purple and silver distin-

guish the bigger Tiger 100.

Unit construction of engine and gear box gives Group B—the big 649 c.c. Thunderbird, Trophy and Bonneville twins—a new sleekness of line which, as on the pair of Tiger sportsters, is assisted by the transfer of the twin contact-breaker assembly to the timing cover.

Bore and stroke dimensions, and many of the internals, remain unaltered. There is, however, a new light-alloy cylinder head with increased fin area, and the finning is extended to the rocker-box castings.

Extra rigidity results from a wider spacing of the cylinder barrel and cylinder head bolts and studs, the revised layout permitting the

introduction of an additional cylinder-head bolt.

The duplex primary chain, with slipper tensioner, transmits the drive to a redesigned clutch. With the object of

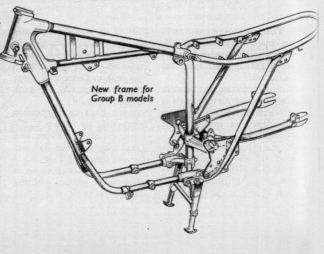

New frame for Group B models

Make / Model	CAPACITY, BORE, STROKE AND TYPE OF ENGINE	CR	IGNITION	GEAR RATIOS				CAPACITY		SUSP		SIZE OF TYRES		Wt lb	PRICE WITH TAX		
				TOP	THIRD	SECOND	BOTTOM	FUEL	OIL	FRONT	REAR	FRONT	REAR		£	s	d
T20 Tiger Cub ...	199 c.c. (63×64mm) o.h.v.	7	C	6.84	9.04	14.05	20.4	3g	2½pt	T	PF	3.25×17	3.25×17	215	166	4	0
T20 S/H Cub Sports...	199 c.c. (63×64mm) o.h.v.	9	C	7.13	8.56	13.37	19.8	3g	2½pt	T	PF	3.00×19	3.50×18	223	188	8	0
TR20 Cub Trials ...	199 c.c. (63×64mm) o.h.v.	7	C	9.15	13.25	20.33	30.1	2⅜g	2½pt	T	PF	2.75×21	4.00×18	212	199	16	0
TS20 Cub Scrambler	199 c.c. (63×64mm) o.h.v.	9	C	9.15	10.93	14.27	18.85	2⅜g	2½pt	T	PF	2.75×21	3.50×19	208	194	8	0
3TA Twenty One ...	349 c.c. (58.25×65.5mm) o.h.v. twin	7.5	C	5.33	6.32	9.37	12.96	3g	5pt	T	PF	3.25×17	3.50×17	340	261	0	0
T90 Tiger 90 ...	349 c.c. (58.25×65.5mm) o.h.v. twin	9	C	6.04	7.15	9.8	14.67	3g	5pt	T	PF	3.25×18	3.50×18	336	274	4	0
5TA Speed Twin ...	490 c.c. (69×65.5mm) o.h.v. twin	7	C	5.05	6	8.88	12.28	3g	5pt	T	PF	3.25×17	3.50×17	341	274	4	0
T100 Tiger 100 ...	490 c.c. (69×65.5mm) o.h.v. twin	9	C	5.7	6.75	9.26	13.86	3g	5pt	T	PF	3.25×18	3.50×18	336	279	0	0
6T Thunderbird ...	649 c.c. (71×82mm) o.h.v. twin	7.5	C	4.6	5.47	7.77	11.43	4g	5pt	T	PF	3.25×18	3.50×18	369	286	4	0
TR6 Trophy ...	649 c.c. (71×82mm) o.h.v. twin	8.5	C	4.84	5.76	8.17	11.81	4g	5pt	T	PF	3.25×19	4.00×18	363	303	0	0
T120 Bonneville 120...	649 c.c. (71×82mm) o.h.v. twin	8.5	C	4.84	5.76	8.17	11.81	4g	5pt	T	PF	3.25×18	3.50×18	363	318	0	0
Tina Scooter ...	99.75 c.c. (50.4×50mm) t.s.	7	M	5	Variable		14.75	1½g	—	TL	PA	3.50×8	3.50×8	140	94	10	0
TS1 Tigress ...	173 c.c. (61.5×58mm) t.s.	7.4	M	4.55	5.81	9.1	13.6	1½g	—	TA	PA	3.50×10	3.50×10	220	152	17	0
TW2 Tigress ...	249 c.c. (56×50.6mm) o.h.v. twin	6.5	C	4	5.2	8	12	1½g	2½pt	TA	PA	3.50×10	3.50×10	240	184	10	0
TW2S Tigress ...	249 c.c. (56×50.6mm) o.h.v. twin	6.5	C	4	5.2	8	12	1½g	2½pt	TA	PA	3.50×10	3.50×10	250	198	0	0

MANUFACTURERS: *Triumph Engineering Co., Ltd., Meriden Works, Allesley, Coventry.*
EXTRAS: *Prop stand, £1 4s 8d; pillion footrests, £1 4s; quickly detachable rear wheel, £4 9s 5d; steering-head lock, 16s 3d; rev-meter and drive (Sports Cub, Tiger 90, Tiger 100, Trophy and Bonneville) £7 16s.*
ABBREVIATIONS: *CR, compression ratio; C, coil; M, magneto; T, telescopic fork; PF, pivoted fork; TL, trailing link; TA, telescopic arm; PA, pivoted arm.*

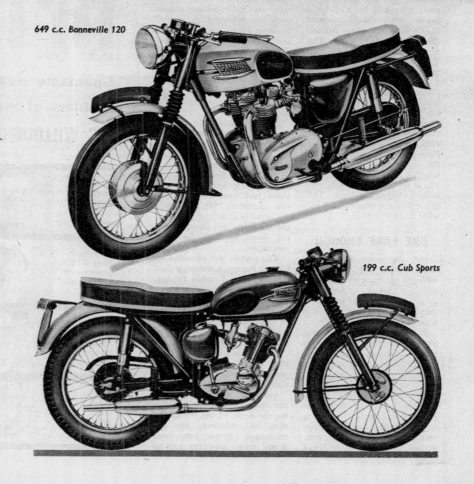

649 c.c. Bonneville 120

199 c.c. Cub Sports

section fairing similar to that of the Tiger sportsters. Oil tank and battery are rubber mounted, as also is the fuel tank—a smart new tank with indents at the rear to accommodate the larger-than-before knee grips. Twin exhausts are fitted.

Genuine roadburners, the Trophy and Bonneville twins differ mainly in that a single carburettor is employed for the Trophy, twin Amals for the Bonnie.

Another identifying point is that the Trophy has a siamesed exhaust system, while the companion model has twin pipes.

Colours? Black and silver for the Thunderbird, regal purple and silver for the Trophy, Alaskan white, with black and gold lining, for the Bonneville.

No change is made to the scooter range, which comprises the 99.75 c.c. Tina (with automatic transmission) and the three Tigress models. The 173 c.c. Tigress is a single-cylinder two-stroke while the remaining pair are two-fifty o.h.v. twins, with and without electric starting.

THE 200 MILE AMA CLASSIC WINNER
DAYTONA

It was a Triumph Tiger 100 which carried Buddy Elmore to victory in the 1966 200 Mile National Championship Road Race at Daytona, Florida.

This race is America's toughest road racing event of the competition year, and Elmore set a scorching new race record of 96·582 m.p.h., almost two m.p.h. faster than the previous record – and this on a machine basically similar to any T100 in your local dealer's showroom.

MOUNTAIN CUB T20|M

200 c.c. O.H.V. SINGLE CYLINDER.

A truly fine lightweight trail bike. The Mountain Cub will take you up hills, over dusty trails, into the back country. A favorite for hunters and fishermen because it gets them where it's tough to go. It can crawl at a snail's pace, yet accelerate to 60 m.p.h. and turn on a dime. There's a 4-speed, special wide ratio gearbox for tractor-like performance in rough going and a regular fourth gear for highway cruising without troublesome chain or sprocket changing. The Cub is the only fully equipped, standard trail bike with no extras to buy. All good reasons to buy one !

FOR SPECIFICATIONS AND TECHNICAL DATA SEE PAGES 10 AND 11

Triumphs for 1965.

John Hartle winning the inaugural Production TT, 1967.

Overhauling a T100, 1962.

King of cool Steve McQueen, 1969.

A hard day's night?

At the 1966 Earls Court show, Robert Leppin poses in Gyronaut X-1, on which he set a world two-wheel speed record of 245.667mph. Power was by two Bonnie engines.

Bonnie publicity picture, 1965.

Super Value from the very centre of England—

1701

..... the **new**

TRIUMPH

SUPER CUB 200

£184.2.1

MANUFACTURER'S RECOMMENDED RETAIL PRICE
INCLUDING PURCHASE TAX AND 10% SURCHARGE

Here's a sparkling new addition to the Triumph range—the Super Cub 200—an attractive new version of the popular Tiger Cub.

It's nippy, easy to handle, economical to run, and in its new <u>Flamboyant Bushfire Red</u>, even more appealing in appearance than its predecessor.

Modern style petrol tank, chromium-plated headlamp, full-width hubs, new type dual seat with safety strap—these are new features which make the Super Cub super value.

USÉ

The Super Cub, 1967.

3-POT

Charles Deane rides and reports this new 130 mph Triumph

▶ **What a fantastic machine! From a standing start to 100 mph and back in approximately 600 yards, plus a top speed of 130 mph through the electronic timing gear!**

For sheer performance, I can think of only one other standard, over-the-counter bike to approach the long awaited three-cylinder Triumph.

My first introduction to the Trident was on a high-speed test strip. I watched the works' test rider hurtle through the timing trap at 129 mph in one direction and 124.8 the other way. He then reeled off two standing quarter-miles with terminal speeds of 105.5 and 102.6 mph.

Then, it was my turn. Having never ridden this giant of a machine, I nervously swung a leg across the saddle. A gentle push on the kick-start and the three cylinders burbled into life.

"Take her to 8000 in the gears and just let her go in top. By the way, you'll have to stop pretty smartly at the end of the strip,

once you are through the lights!"

Pulling in the surprisingly light clutch, I snicked the bike into first gear. The movement was so easy and clonk-free that I had to check to make sure it was in gear.

As I slowly rode away with the motor barely ticking over, I carried out a quick check of all controls for adjustment and positioning. Satisfied that everything was working properly, I rode to the end of the test strip, quickly getting the feel of the Trident.

The gearchanges were smooth and positive and the three carburettors were very responsive to the throttle.

Steering was light and once on the move, the 460 lb. of machinery appeared no greater burden on the rider than any other big bike. It could be trickled along at walking pace with perfect balance and under complete control.

The riding position was comfortable with the wide bars giving

Neat and uncluttered, the tachometer and speedometer units with ammeter, main beam and ignition warning lights. Note steering lock

The oil cooler is necessary to keep the 3-cylinder motor cool. In fact, it is so efficient, the temperature is lower than twins

Triple coils, condensers and the relay for the twin-windtone horns are situated neatly beneath the dual seat alongside oil filler cap

The triple Amal concentric carbs are close-coupled with rubber mountings to the cylinder heads. Note the single large air filter

32

MOTORCYCLE MECHANICS

TRIDENT

an almost armchair position on the well-upholstered dual-seat. Even my 29 in. inside leg could easily reach the ground without trouble.

The brakes had been tested to their limits on the previous high-speed runs and before I blasted down the timing strip, I made a quick adjustment of the front twin-leading-shoe stopper at the handlebar lever.

The thin ribbon of tarmac stretched before me with the electronic timing gear just visible almost three-quarters of a mile away.

Winding up the motor to about 4000 rpm, I dropped the clutch in first gear with a minimum of slip. As the revs dropped briefly and the power came in at about 3000 rpm, the brute of a machine rapidly surged forward.

Hanging desperately on to the handlebars and with knees slipping from their grip on the fuel tank, I struggled to reach the clutch lever and hook my toes under the gear change lever

as the revs rapidly built up to the 8000 mark.

At about 50 in first, I lifted the gear lever into second and dropped the clutch with full throttle on all three carbs. With crash helmet pulling my head back and still struggling to retain my hold on the tank with my knees, the bike hurtled towards the 80 mark on the speedometer.

With such vivid acceleration, the most difficult thing was reaching for the clutch and hooking a toe under the gear-lever. It felt as though an invisible giant was trying to lift you backwards off the bike!

With power coming in hard in the middle of the power band, I changed into third and, once again, just hung on till I saw the needle on the rev counter reading a rapid 8000.

Then, with relief, I hooked the gear-lever into top, put my feet on the pillion footrests, wrapped myself around the tank and screamed towards the timing lights.

Jet-styling for the silencers give the three-cylinder a distinctive appearance. Exhaust note was very subdued, even at high engine speed

The view which most other cars and bikes will have of the new Triumph. The Dunlop K81 was the tyre especially designed for Trident

DECEMBER, 1968

105

TRIUMPH TRIDENT

MM SUPER TEST

3-POT POWER

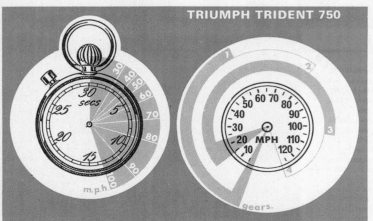

TRIUMPH TRIDENT 750

Performance

Speeds in gears:

	Minimum	Maximum
1st	2	55
2nd	6	80
3rd	14	104
4th	22	129

Acceleration:

0–30	2.4 sec.	0–40	3.4 sec.
0–50	4.2 sec.	0–60	5.4 sec.
0–70	7.0 sec.	0–80	8.8 sec.
0–90	11.6 sec.	0–100	13.4 sec.

Standing quarter-mile covered in 13.4 sec. with terminal speed of 105.5 mph.

Fuel consumption:

High speed motorcycling	34 mpg
Touring with 70 limit	54 mpg
About town riding	50 mpg
Average	46 mpg

Braking:
Braking from 30 mph on dry tarmac—32 ft. 6 in. (11-stone rider).

Specifications

Engine:
740 cc (bore and stroke—67 x 70 mm) overhead valve, transverse three cylinders. Maximum claimed output, 58 bhp at 7500 rpm. Compression ratio 9 to 1. Dry sump lubrication. Bearings: ball on driving side, roller on timing, with two plain main inner bearings; plain big-ends.

Carburation:
Three Amal concentric 626 with 27 mm diameter chokes; air slides operated by handlebar lever. Also, single large felt-and-mesh air filter.

Transmission:
Primary: $\frac{3}{8}$ in. triplex chain in oil-bath case with adjustable tensioner. Secondary: single $\frac{5}{8}$ x $\frac{3}{8}$ in. chain. Four-speed foot operated gearbox, ratios: 11.95, 8.3, 5.83 and 4.87 to 1. Clutch: single plate Borg and Beck diaphragm unit.

Electrical Equipment:
Ignition: battery, triple contact breaker and coils. Charging: Lucas 110 watt alternator through rectifier and zener diode to 8 amp-hour battery. Lighting: Lucas 7 in. headlamp with rear stoplight operated by both front and rear brake.

Suspension:
Telescopic front fork with two-way damping. Swinging arm rear with three-position Girling suspension units.

Brakes:
8 in. twin-leading-shoe front and 7 in. single-leading-shoe rear.

Capacities:
Oil—$5\frac{1}{2}$ pints, including oil cooler. Fuel—$4\frac{1}{4}$ gallons.

Dimensions:
Wheelbase, 58 in. Saddle height, 32 in. Ground clearance, $6\frac{1}{2}$ in. Weight, 468 lb.

Price: To be announced.

Manufacturers: Triumph Engineering Co Ltd, Meriden, Coventry, Warks.

I watched the rev counter climb up to 8000 and then beyond! It was showing just on 8400 as I flashed through the speed trap—a speed of 125.7 mph.

I then discovered why one had to stop rapidly after the trap—with almost 7 cwt. of man and machine hurtling along at almost 130 mph, 300 yards are soon covered in braking.

Standing and pulling on both front and rear brakes, I just managed to stop the mighty Trident before the end of the strip.

I must admit, I was very thankful for those new twin-leading-shoe Triumph brakes and the effective, fade-free results they achieve.

A repeat performance in the opposite direction and then a standing-quarter with a terminal speed of 102 mph proved to me that this new three-cylinder Triumph is the fastest standard roadster yet produced by the BSA/Triumph group.

At the end of this hard day's testing, the Triumph wasn't any the worse for wear and not a sign of oil leaked from the 58 bhp motor. It ticked over smoothly and gave no impression that it had just completed a series of racing speed tests.

The only vibration felt at the handlebars was between 5500 and 6400 rpm and this was no more than a tremor. Throughout the rest of the rev range, the motor was incredibly smooth.

Fuel consumption figures for these top speed tests were pretty shattering with a mere 32 to 34 mpg being registered.

But, on the road, after a brief overnight run to London and then back to the Meriden Triumph factory, I averaged a more respectable 52 to 56 mpg.

Cruising down the motorway at 70 mph was virtually a doddle, with the engine ticking over at approximately 4500 rpm. On the test circuit, the Trident is one of the few bikes I have ridden where, at 90 mph you open the throttle and still get "hit in the back" with the acceleration.

Handling up to the 70 legal limit is perfect, but I found that there is still a sign of the rear-end weaving when on full bore in a straight line and also, when you shut off on long, fast bends.

About town the Trident was impeccable with its docile, tractable motor. A mere whiff of throttle kept the well-silenced three-cylinder waffling along at 30 mph in top, although it is better to ride in third gear for rapid overtaking.

With triple-coil ignition, the three-cylinder was never any problem to start. A simple flooding of the outside two carbs and with ignition on, it only required the slightest of prods on the kick-start to set the motor in motion.

The electrics are all 12-volt and lighting is perfectly adequate for normal touring speeds at night.

There's no doubt that the Triumph 3-pot is the machine I would like to have as my high-speed tourer. But with a proposed price of around £550, it's certainly an expensive lot for the average rider. ●

MOTORCYCLE MECHANICS

34

Craig Vetter styled X75 Hurricane three.

Dave Croxford – partnered by Alex George – won the 1975 Production TT on 'Slippery Sam', the famous racing Trident. 'Sam' was a TT winner five times in a row, this year the last.

Ride like the law, 1972.

Arthur Browning, TR5T, causes a splash during the 1971 ISDT.

The UK spec Jubilee Bonnie.

US version of the same.

RIDE A LIVING LEGEND
TRIUMPH

Certificate of Ownership

This is to certify that

_____

is the Owner of a Triumph Silver 750, one of a thousand special versions of the Triumph Bonneville 750 motorcycle manufactured as a Limited Edition by Meriden Motorcycles Limited for sale in the United Kingdom, in honour of the Silver Jubilee of the reign of Her Majesty Queen Elizabeth II

SPECIMEN ONLY

Chairman,
Meriden Motorcycles Limited

Authorised Triumph Dealer
Date

Silver 750 Limited Edition

Jubilee certificate.

Head down for Ray Pickrell, Trident, at the 1972 Race of the Year, Mallory Park.

Home market Bonneville for 1980.

Bonnie bend swinging, 1979.

Bonneville T140E (S) Special Police Motorcycle

Last of the police line, the 1981 T140ES.

As the 80s dawned Triumph was, to put it bluntly, on its knees. Though there had been various attempts at new models – like the eight-valve TSS and the 'factory customs' (which, incidentally, though started by Triumph with the Hurricane had been wholly embraced by the Japanese) – there was nothing really 'new'. By the start of 1983, manufacture at Meriden had altogether ground to a halt and the end looked nigh for a company which 15 or so years earlier had, in the Bonneville, been building arguably the most well-known, desirable motorcycle in the world. Just a decade and a half earlier, Triumphs had been beloved of rock stars, movie icons and the motorcycling public – now, as the 80s began, the company and its products appeared a relic of an era no one was interested in. It was, indeed, a rapid fall from grace.

With Triumph now broke and out of business, it was in late 1983 that a new name entered the rich history of Triumph. John Bloor, building magnate and entrepreneur, bought the name, all existing projects, the logos, the trademarks and everything else associated with the company. It may have seemed a strange decision to those looking on as Bloor had no history in motorcycling, or indeed even engineering, but he had proved himself a shrewd and successful businessman.

Meanwhile, the Triumph name didn't completely disappear, as John Bloor licensed out the rights to build twins to Les Harris, who continued to make a small, but steady, stream of Bonnevilles, while Mr Bloor set about resurrecting the Triumph concern proper. A factory – built by Bloor's own company, naturally – was constructed on

1982 Bonneville Royal, at Meriden.

a 10-acre greenfield site on the outskirts of Hinckley. In the early days, though, there were no great proclamations about when, what or where Triumph was going to concentrate its efforts. Indeed the building of the factory had been completed in a quiet, unobtrusive manner and

it was 1988 when the motorcycle world really noticed that Bloor had completed his factory. Still, the project was swathed in secrecy and no one was prepared to spill Bloor's secrets.

The first clue that things were happening was when in 1988, at a convention in the US, some castings were displayed – but that was it. With the British motorcycling press itching to know more, still mystery and secrecy shrouded the whole enterprise – the message was clear; we'll tell you when we're good and ready.

The moment finally came in 1990 when at the Cologne Motorshow, in Germany, the range of three and four-cylinder machines was shown and again, soon after, at the Milan, Italy, show. Though the models were clearly influenced by Japanese machines – and some aimed barbed comments – the simple reality was Triumph had looked at what was being made and decided to not over complicate, or over stretch things. The old adage of not running before one can walk, seemed to hold true – and very sensible it seemed too.

From 1982, the T140ES has more than a hint of BMW's successful R90/100S about it...

The reintroduced Thunderbird name – a single carb 750 twin.

The bright new hope, the eight-valve TSS.

Early 80s Tiger Trail was the last in a long line of off-road ohv twins.

TS8-1, an attempt at updating.

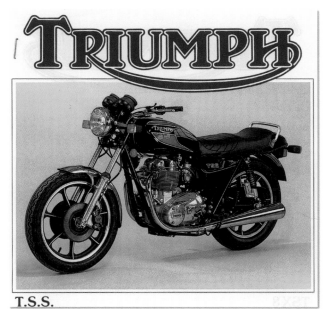

T.S.S.

1983 TSS.

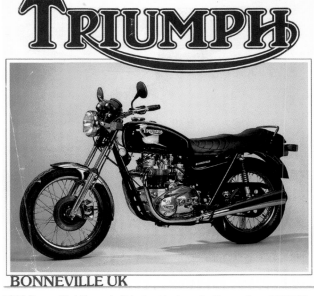

BONNEVILLE UK

1983 Bonneville UK – as built by Les Harris under licence from 1985-88.

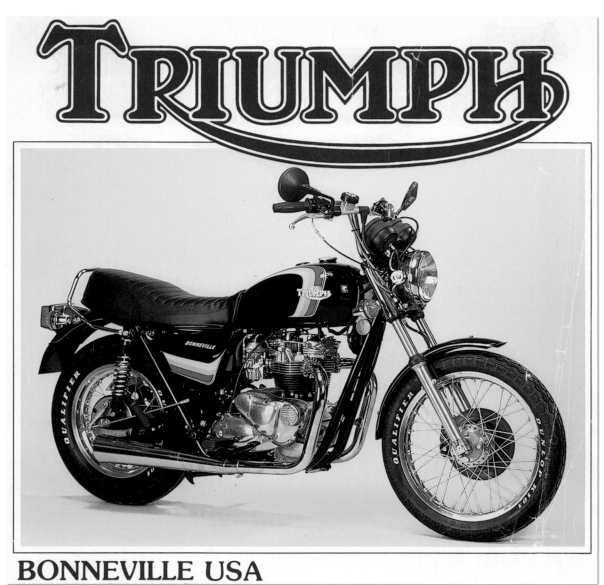

BONNEVILLE USA

1983 Bonneville US.

Early 750cc prototype Trident, as unveiled to the world's press in autumn 1990.

TSS on the move.

The shape of things to come – the Phoenix 900, May 1983.

Getting established
1991-2000

1991 Daytona 750.

In 1991, brand new, freshly designed motorcycles bearing the Triumph name appeared in dealer showrooms for the first time in years. By April, some models were on sale and by September, the full range was available. Canny businessman that he is, Bloor had realised that he needed to have the trust and support of the retail industry if his venture even had a chance of succeeding. To that end, a whole dealer network had been set up – and assured that the product they were going to get to sell would be well-made and the dealer wouldn't find itself correcting basic problems which were the fault of the factory; sadly, something that had been a major problem at the end of the Meriden days. The fact that Bloor was prepared to go to these lengths meant that the dealers had faith in him and his product – a great basis on which to start a working relationship.

The initial 'relaunch' models didn't attempt to be anything particularly revolutionary or even evocative of what had gone before – it was just a case of establishing a foothold in the market. To that end, Triumph went

1994 Tiger 900.

1994 Daytona 900.

1994 Thunderbird.

for a modular concept, with a six-model launch range which consisted of the Trident 750 and 900, Daytona 750 and 1000 and Trophy 900 and 1200. The 750 and 900cc models were all triples, with the 1000 and 1200 versions four cylinder. However, all models shared the same chassis, fuel tanks, engine components (and cylinder bore) and running gear while subtle differences in wheelbase were attributed to different length forks and suspensions variations. It had been decided that it was crucial to Triumph establishing an identity that there was a three in the range – again, reasoning which proved sound, as it is unquestionably for its triples which Triumph is best known today.

The early models quickly proved popular and gained a reputation for being 'overbuilt' – Bloor and his team didn't want to upset those dealers to whom they'd promised that the new models would be of a high quality and to that end Triumph had over-engineered in the interest of strength and reliability,

shrewdly reasoning it would be a good reputation to establish.

It soon became apparent that triples would be the future and more cylinder models appeared, with the off-road Tiger and 'semi-sports' Sprint – a halfway house between the Trident and the Trophy. But, cried many, where were machines to appear to the 'traditionalist' – and where were the most famous names from the Triumph portfolio?

The first answer came with the Thunderbird, launched for 1995, joined soon after by the similarly styled Adventurer. It marked a clear new direction for Triumph, possibly moving away from where the restart had begun and into different territory. Also launched for 1995 was the 'naked' musclebike, the Speed Triple.

For 1997, came a new direction of sportsters, the T595 Daytona and the T509 Speed Triple, with redesigned Trophies, Sprints, Tigers and a new 600 four, the TT600, all added to the range. The game was on.

Multi world champion Phil Read on a Speed Triple, Mallory Park, Past Masters Race 1997.

Trophy 1200, 1992.

Speed Triple racer on the Triumph stand, 1994 Sporting Show.

New generation Trophy 1200, 1996.

1999 Daytona 955i.

Trophy 900 by the dock of the bay, 1991.

Chapter

12 **Onwards and upwards**
2001-2010

2008 Sprint ST on the move.

It had to happen — it was just a case of when. The 'when will it be?' moment had been speculated on ever since the first new Triumph had appeared and, for 2001, the famous Bonneville name was once more in the Triumph range. Aimed squarely at the retro market, the reborn Bonneville was however a fully modern motorcycle. Powered by a 790cc parallel twin, the Bonneville was not supposed to be the rip snorting sportster its original forebear had been but was instead an all round more friendly motorcycle, with looks that aped the original. Although some were disappointed,

others immediately understood what the Bonneville was — an alternative to a certain motorcycle from Milwaukee that had done okay over the years, as well as a rival to the Japanese made retros and cruisers. And of course this one had Triumph written on the petrol tank.

The Bonneville has remained a mainstay of the Triumph range, with the firm realising that the base model could be developed to fill other niches, hence the launch of the Thruxton cafe racer version (2003) and the Scrambler (2005), while the more powerful

The late Craig Jones on the Valmoto Triumph. 'Jonesy' won the last race of the 2003 Supersport calendar, his – and Triumph's – only win of the year.

Sprint RS, 2003.

865cc engine eventually found its way into the basic Bonneville. For 2008 there was a further advance for the Bonnevilles when they were switched to fuel injection. However, the early 'noughties' wasn't all plain sailing as in 2002 the Hinckley plant was subject to a potentially devastating fire, and though production was massively disrupted Triumph was soon back, stronger than ever. New models continued to come apace. In the ultra-competitive 600cc supersports class, the initial TT600 was replaced by a more focused machine, the Daytona 600.

The angular race-rep immediately found favour, while Triumph made a return to racing with the model in 2003, with the Valmoto team. Though success didn't come immediately, Triumph did claim a first TT win since the days of Slippery Sam when Kiwi Bruce Anstey took the Junior 600cc race. In the British championship, Scotsman Jim Moodie and young Englishman Craig Jones thrilled race fans with Jones claiming a victory at Donington Park – the team's last race as Triumph withdrew at season's end. There were plenty of other ground-breaking new models through the noughties too, with the awesome Rocket III (2300cc, three cylinders, masses of torque) illustrating Triumph's willingness to plough its own furrow. Another example of that individuality ethos was the 675cc Daytona. This machine was another competitor in the supersport 600 category — but while the earlier Daytona 600 went along the same lines as the Japanese, this one was all Triumph's own thinking. And it proved an immense hit — on the

It had to come – the new Bonneville, out for the year 2001.

roads, and on the racetracks too, with in 2008 Aussies Garry McCoy and Mark Aitchison carrying the fight at World Supersports level, with their compatriot Glen Richards winning the prestigious and competitive British Supersport championship that year, winning four out of 12 races, and finishing in every outing. In 2009, McCoy finished on the podium in world level races, then Chaz Davies was fourth in the world, in 2010.

In 2010, the Tiger 800 – an off-road styled triple – was launched, and Triumph ended the decade as a real force, competing across several different sectors of the motorcycling market.

T100 Bonneville in the snow, Christmas 2005.

2008 Tiger.

Norman Hyde Bonnie, 2007.

The aftermath of the devastating 2002 fire.

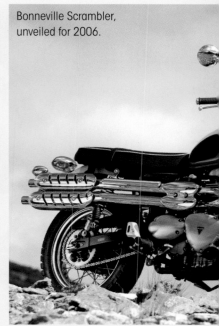

Bonneville Scrambler, unveiled for 2006.

Bonneville America, 2002.

TT600, 2002.

Thruxton Bonnie at the Ace Cafe, 2004.

2006 Daytona 675.

2002 Daytona 955i.

2019 Scrambler XE.

Happy scramblers, in big (1200) and small (900) configurations.

Sharp-handling and super torquey 1200cc Thruxton.

World champion at Moto2, 2019, Alex Marquez at speed. His chassis was made by German company Kalex, with Triumph power.